The Black Archive #15
FULL CIRCLE

By John Toon

Published January 2018 by Obverse Books

Cover Design © Cody Schell

Text © John Toon, 2018

Range Editors: James Cooray Smith, Philip Purser-Hallard

John would like to thank:

Phil and Jim for all of their encouragement, suggestions and feedback; Andrew Smith for kindly giving up his time to discuss some of the points raised in this book; Matthew Kilburn for using his access to the Bodleian Library to help me with my citations; Jo Toon and Darusha Wehm for beta reading my first draft; and Jo again for giving me the support and time to work on this book.

2

For you. Yes, you! Go on, you deserve it.

Also Available

CONTENTS

OVERVIEW

Serial Title: *Full Circle*

Writer: Andrew Smith

Director: Peter Grimwade

Original UK Transmission Dates: 25 October 1980 – 15 November 1980

Running Time:　　　Episode 1: 24m 27s

　　　　　　　　　　　Episode 2: 22m 15s

　　　　　　　　　　　Episode 3: 22m 0s

　　　　　　　　　　　Episode 4: 24m 19s

UK Viewing Figures: Episode 1: 5.9 million

　　　　　　　　　　　Episode 2: 3.7 million

　　　　　　　　　　　Episode 3: 5.9 million

　　　　　　　　　　　Episode 4: 5.5 million

Regular Cast: Tom Baker (Doctor Who), Lalla Ward (Romana), Matthew Waterhouse (Adric), John Leeson (Voice of K-9)

Guest Cast: George Baker (Login), Leonard Maguire (Draith), James Bree (Nefred), Alan Rowe (Garif), Tony Calvin (Dexeter), Richard Willis (Varsh), Bernard Padden (Tylos), June Page (Keara), Andrew Forbes (Omril), Adrian Gibbs (Rysik), Barney Lawrence (Marshman), Norman Bacon (Marshchild)

Antagonists: Marshmen

Novelisation: *Doctor Who: Full Circle* by Andrew Smith. **The Target**

Doctor Who Library #26.

Sequels and Prequels: *State of Decay* (TV, 1980), *Warriors' Gate* (TV, 1981)[1], *Mistfall* (audio, 2015), 'A Full Life' (audio short story, 2016).

Responses:

'A stylish and confident story, saddled with an irritating gang of youths (of which Matthew Waterhouse is the least offensive) and a confused resolution.'

[Mark Campbell, *Doctor Who: The Episode Guide*, p161]

'*Full Circle* is a return to form for Season Eighteen, benefiting from a rewardingly complex plot and generally excellent acting and production...'

[Paul Clarke, *Doctor Who Reviews*]

---

[1] *Full Circle* and these stories make up the so-called 'E-space Trilogy', but see Chapter 1.

SYNOPSIS

Episode 1

Answering a Time Lord summons[2], the TARDIS encounters a baffling disruption, bringing **the Doctor, Romana** and **K-9** to a marshy world which – despite what the scanner shows – is definitely not Gallifrey.

Outside, the people of Alzarius have their own concerns. Decider **Draith** and the scientist **Dexeter** examine a harvest of riverfruit for evidence of the anomalous insect life said to prefigure a recurring natural disaster called Mistfall; while **Adric**, a young mathematical prodigy, tries to join his older brother **Varsh**'s gang of cave-dwelling outcasts, the Outlers, who reject Mistfall as propaganda.

When vapours rise from the water and Mistfall begins, the locals – the braver Outlers excepted – hurry to wait out the danger in their ancestors' crashed Starliner. At the river Draith sees Adric stealing riverfruit for the Outlers and implores him to come with them, but Adric struggles and hurts him. Draith tells Adric that 'we've come full circle,' before being pulled underwater by unseen forces.

At the Starliner, with Draith's return in doubt, his fellow Deciders **Nefred** and **Garif** discuss the question of his successor, while **Login**, the father of the Outler **Keara**, fears for his daughter's safety. In the mist, the injured Adric stumbles into the TARDIS, where the Doctor has formed a troubling suspicion that they are outside real space altogether. Leaving Romana and Adric in the TARDIS while they explore, the Doctor and K-9 see menacing amphibious figures rising out of the marsh.

---

[2] Received at the end of *Meglos* (1980) episode 4.

8

Episode 2

Adric, recovered with surprising speed from his wound, returns to warn his brother and friends of the danger of Mistfall. At their insistence, he reluctantly leads them to the TARDIS, which they attempt to hijack. The Doctor and K-9 watch as the **Marshmen** acclimatise themselves to life on land. Sending K-9 to follow the creatures, the Doctor returns to the TARDIS, but it is gone – carried by Marshmen, with Romana and the Outlers inside, to the Outlers' own cave for use as a battering ram against the Starliner.

Aboard the ship Nefred, Draith's successor as First Decider, is troubled by the secret knowledge he has gained from the Starliner's System Files. He and Garif admit to Login, now appointed as the third of their triumvirate, that the story that the mist outside is toxic is propaganda, meaning that Keara may survive. Nefred restates the Deciders' promise to the people that a repaired Starliner will one day return their descendants to their original home planet of Terradon. The Doctor breaks into the sealed starship, inadvertently letting in a juvenile Marshman who has been following him. Both are captured and brought before the Deciders, who hand the **Marshchild** over to Dexeter before quizzing the Doctor about what he learned from Adric of Draith's death.

In the cave, Romana and the Outlers are besieged by the Marshmen until K-9 arrives, but the creatures attack and incapacitate him. Sometime later, though, they leave suddenly. Emerging to investigate, the TARDIS' occupants discover that this is because of the huge **spiders** hatching from the Outlers' contraband riverfruit. The Outlers flee into the TARDIS, which Adric inadvertently causes to dematerialise – leaving Romana behind to be bitten by a spider.

Episode 3

The TARDIS brings the Outlers to the Starliner, and the Doctor and Adric travel back to the cave to rescue Romana and K-9. They find the former unconscious, and the latter missing his head. They bring them and some dead spiders back to the Starliner.

Meanwhile the Deciders rule that the Outlers are to be pardoned, and allowed to rejoin their parents' society with no punishment. They also authorise Dexeter to begin invasive experiments on the Marshchild, which the Doctor and Adric arrive in time to witness. As Dexeter begins surgery on the creature's brain, Romana wakes screaming in the TARDIS, her face covered in glittering vein-like lines. The Marshchild escapes its restraints and wrecks the lab, killing Dexeter, but on seeing the Doctor on a two-way observation screen, it tries to reach him by smashing the screen and electrocutes itself.

The Doctor is furious at the Marshchild's death, and holds Nefred responsible – for this, and for his deception of the populace. Nefred admits that the Starliner has been repaired and ready to fly for centuries, but rejects the Doctor's accusation that the Deciders have deliberately prolonged their own power. In fact, the information about how to launch the Starliner was lost in the crash.

Adric brings the news that Romana has disappeared from the TARDIS, her room smashed up just like Dexeter's lab. She is, in fact, busy at an emergency escape hatch, letting in the Marshmen.

Episode 4

The Marshmen overrun the Starliner, adapting quickly to their new environment. The Doctor retrieves K-9's head from a Marshman's club, and wears it as a mask to intimidate a group of them, including Romana. The Deciders dither until the Marshmen arrive in their sanctum. Nefred is mortally wounded as they flee. His last words reveal why their people can never return to Terradon: 'Because we have never been there.'

Having noticed Adric's accelerated healing, the Doctor examines cell samples from a spider, the Marshchild and the late Dexeter, and finds that they have the same structure. He creates a serum which cures Romana of her spider-venom infection, returning her to her right mind. He also determines empirically that pure oxygen can repel the Marshmen, who cannot adapt quickly enough to the change in atmosphere. The Outlers fight them using oxygen cylinders, but Varsh is killed protecting Adric. Login helps the Doctor flood the Starliner with oxygen, expelling all the Marshmen.

The Doctor explains that the Starliner's original occupants are extinct: the current population are descended from Marshmen who overran the starship many millennia ago, and have since adapted to resemble, and to believe themselves, its natural inhabitants. He and Romana show the remaining Deciders how to launch the Starliner, and after some prevarication, they do so.

Back aboard the TARDIS, the Doctor and Romana find a gift from Adric[3]: an image translator from Dexeter's microscope, which because it was produced locally will allow the scanner to see the true outside.

The Doctor tells Romana and a repaired K-9 that the disturbance

---

[3] Adric has also hidden aboard the TARDIS, a fact not revealed until *State of Decay* episode 1.

they encountered (a 'charged vacuum emboitement' or CVE) has taken them into E-Space, outside normal spacetime.

CHAPTER 1: SQUARING THE CIRCLE

There's a line of argument among some **Doctor Who** fans that *Full Circle* (1980) 'is where the John Nathan-Turner era really kicks in'[4]. On the face of it, this is an odd assertion – Nathan-Turner wasted no time in putting his mark on **Doctor Who** when he became the show's producer in 1979 and began preparing its 18th season, and there can be no mistaking the visual, musical and narrative ways in which the opening story of Season 18, *The Leisure Hive* (1980), announces itself as a fresh start for the series.

Moreover, 'the John Nathan-Turner era' isn't a particularly useful way to classify 1980s **Who**. Nathan-Turner produced **Doctor Who** for a full decade, during which time the tone of the show varied substantially, which argues against considering this period of the show as a single cohesive 'era'. Nathan-Turner also had little narrative input into the show: unusually for a BBC producer, his background was not in directing or script editing but as a production manager with a particular focus on budgetary matters. His involvement in some casting decisions and his high-level requests that certain elements be written into scripts undoubtedly had an impact on the tone of **Doctor Who**, but his direct influence on the scripts is minor[5]. It's arguably more meaningful to discuss his 'era' in terms of the three script editors who tried to define its narrative direction during their tenure – earnest Christopher H

---

[4] Miles, Lawrence, and Tat Wood, *About Time: The Unauthorized Guide to Doctor Who #5 – 1980-1984: Seasons 18 to 21* (2005), p42.
[5] Let's pass quickly over his co-authorship of *Dimensions in Time* (1993) and certain scenes in *The Trial of a Time Lord* (1986), on the strength of which scriptwriting wasn't his forte.

Bidmead (1980-81), grim and gritty Eric Saward (1982-86), and the more whimsically dark Andrew Cartmel (1987-89)[6].

So is *Full Circle* where the Christopher H Bidmead era kicks in? Even this is pushing it given that *Full Circle* was the fourth story of Season 18 in production order, fully halfway through Bidmead's short tenure as script editor. Besides, it's easy enough to spot his input into the transmitted scripts for *The Leisure Hive*, *State of Decay* and *Meglos* (all 1980), if only by contrast with the other influences in those scripts. What can be said about *Full Circle* is that it's the first story in Season 18 to really put his vision of **Doctor Who** front and centre. Preceded in production order by stories that were commissioned and scripted in rushed circumstances and followed by stories over which Bidmead had more direct control, *Full Circle* marks the tipping point in shaking off the lingering influence of the previous era – that of producer Graham Williams and script editor Douglas Adams – and establishing Bidmead as the prime authorial influence on the tone of Season 18. It isn't so much 'where the John Nathan-Turner era really kicks in', but rather where the Williams-Adams era really kicks **out**.

Scripting Season 18

When Bidmead took on the job of script editor[7], he found himself in the uncomfortable position of having 'one script on the shelf [and]

---

[6] Perhaps I'm doing a disservice to Antony Root, but with only three **Doctor Who** stories to his name spread out across Season 19, interspersed with stories edited and in two cases also written by Saward, it would be pushing it to list him as a fourth major influence on the tone of 1980s **Who**.

something like a month before we had to get our first script together'[8]. That one existing script was David Fisher's *The Leisure Hive*, which had already been commissioned by Nathan-Turner on 20 December 1979[9]. Work proceeded on that story and on resurrecting Terrance Dicks' 'The Vampire Mutation', eventually retitled *State of Decay*, while Bidmead went in search of scriptwriters for the rest of the season.

Bidmead found *The Leisure Hive* to be 'a strange script, which didn't fully fit in with our premise as it emerged over the season', but was unable to take the time to overhaul it completely as it was 'a rush job in that there were no other usable stories'[10]. The result as broadcast is a halfway house between the lighter 'silly' tone of the previous year championed by Fisher and, in the studio, Tom Baker, and the 'serious' tone the new production team was aiming for – Nathan-Turner's influence comes across loud and clear in the production aspects of the story, but Bidmead's authorial voice is only one among many[11].

---

[7] '[D]uring the first week of January 1980' according to *In-Vision* #46, p5; 'just before Christmas 1979' says Pixley, Andrew, 'DWM Archive: Full Circle', *Doctor Who Magazine* (DWM) #327, p33.

[8] *Myth Makers #87: Christopher H Bidmead*.

[9] Pixley, Andrew, 'Archive Extra', DWM Special Edition #9: *The Complete Fourth Doctor – Volume 2*, p56.

[10] Quoted in DWM Special Edition #16: *In Their Own Words, Volume 3 – 1977-81*, p68.

[11] *In-Vision* #46 claims that 'Bidmead's later contributions were mostly to do with expanding and putting right all the references to tachyonics in the script' (p5).

State of Decay similarly shows its roots in a story idea held over from a previous production regime – in its case, the latter end of the Philip Hinchcliffe / Robert Holmes 'Gothic' era of the series – and it reflects Bidmead's editorial intent even less clearly than *The Leisure Hive*, with director Peter Moffatt actively working to overturn rewrites that both he and Dicks disliked. Moffatt had expressed his interest in directing the story as originally conceived by Dicks, and ultimately succeeded in reverting the shooting script from Bidmead's more science-heavy rewrite to 'the original medieval-style script, albeit with some alterations'[12].

Meglos was the first story of the season to be scripted by writers commissioned by Bidmead – John Flanagan and Andrew McCulloch, both alumni of repertory theatre like Bidmead himself. It's clear from the finished programme that he still hadn't worked out how to get across what he wanted **Doctor Who** under his editorship to look like, while Flanagan and McCulloch were still visibly influenced by the tone of the previous year's season[13]. It's hard to imagine Bidmead, with his love of scientific detail, letting pass this broad tale of the pantomimic conflict between technocratic Savants and

---

[12] As Bidmead recalled, the version finally used 'was Terrance's script, with bits by me' (DWM Special Edition #16, pp75-76).

[13] 'John Flanagan and Andrew McCulloch's stuff didn't chime 100% with my vision for **Doctor Who**, but my vision was very "special", and I wasn't terribly good at conveying it to people!' (DWM Special Edition #16, p71.) In addition, as *In-Vision* #47 reveals, Flanagan and McCulloch's real ambition was to become comedy writers, which would have made them more of a natural fit for the Adams-helmed season 17 than the more straight-faced season 18 (p4).

superstitious Deons and the ancient, mystical, mad science of a power-hungry cactus if he hadn't been so pressed for time.

Still finding his feet as a script editor, not yet able to articulate the direction in which he wanted to steer **Doctor Who**, and under pressure to start lining up material for the cast and crew to work on, Bidmead was evidently on the back foot as far as these first three scripts were concerned. In the case of *State of Decay*, he wasn't merely drowned out by other authorial voices but found himself actually at odds with the writer and director. But the rest of Season 18 finds him far more in control of the programme's tone and content – not only in his own *Logopolis* (1981) but in the other three stories of the season too, all of which, according to his own recollection, he ended up rewriting 'from top to bottom', with or without the collaboration of writers and directors[14]. *Full Circle* marks the turning point in Bidmead's ascendancy as script editor.

Like *State of Decay*, *Full Circle* had its origin in a story proposal – titled 'The Planet That Slept' – that had previously been submitted to the **Doctor Who** production office. Unlike *State of Decay*, it hadn't been taken up for development by the then script editor[15],

---

[14] On *Full Circle*: 'I had to sit down and rewrite that script from top to bottom with, I seem to remember, [writer Andrew Smith's] great help and co-operation' (*Myth Makers* #87). On *Warriors' Gate* (1981): '[T]he fact is that [director Paul Joyce] and I totally rewrote the script from top to bottom' (DWM Special Edition #16, p81). On *The Keeper of Traken* (1981): '[T]his was another show on which I had to shut the doors, sit down and rewrite the script myself from top to bottom', (*Myth Makers* #87 again).
[15] Dicks' 'The Vampire Mutation' had famously been planned for production as part of Season 15 and then shelved to avoid

but it struck a chord with Bidmead, who made contact with writer Andrew Smith. Smith, still only 17 years old when Bidmead first met him, had enjoyed some success contributing sketches to **Not the Nine O'Clock News** (1979-82) and radio programmes including **Week Ending** (1970-98), but had no prior experience as a drama scriptwriter; everything he knew in that field, he'd learnt from Malcolm Hulke's *Writing for Television in the 70s* (1974) and a brief script excerpt in the back of Hulke and Dicks' *The Making of Doctor Who* (1972)[16]. A keen fan of the series, Smith was eager to write for **Doctor Who** and willing to work closely with the script editor, an experience which Bidmead as a novice script editor evidently found stimulating: '[T]his was a guy who was thoroughly on the ball, and I thought, I just want to work with this guy!'[17]

As Smith recalls it, the process of script development was a highly collaborative one, but one in which Bidmead's edits came increasingly to the fore:

> 'After the second draft, Chris produced a draft that had a lot of changes in it [...] It's still very much my story, but it was enough of a change after that second draft that it did kind of take the wind out of my sails [...] Episode 1 is almost entirely

---

undercutting the BBC's high-profile 1977 adaptation of Bram Stoker's *Dracula* starring Louis Jourdan. Regarding Smith's story proposal, Bidmead remembers in the *Full Circle* DVD extra 'All Aboard the Starliner': 'I seem to recall that it had originally been put in front of my predecessor, Douglas Adams, and it hadn't chimed with what he wanted to do, but this piece of paper was still floating around the office.'

[16] *Myth Makers* #122.
[17] 'All Aboard the Starliner'.

mine, and then it drifts, episode 2 is about two thirds and then episode 4 is about 70 percent Chris.'[18]

Having noted that he was taken aback by the changes to his scripts, Smith also observes that 'the same thing was done to other writers that season as well, that tended to be Chris' thing'[19]. This hardly describes Bidmead's editorial work on the scripts that preceded *Full Circle* into production, but certainly applies to those that followed it. We might well imagine that it was the experience of working with Smith that gave Bidmead the confidence to take more of a lead in shaping the latter half of Season 18.

With *Warriors' Gate* (1981), Bidmead would again find himself working with a writer who had experience in other fields but not in televised drama. The issue here was that Stephen Gallagher, primarily a writer of science-fictional horror novels, had overwritten his scripts and hadn't teased out their ideas in a way that would meet the dramatic requirements of television. Bidmead was ultimately obliged to strip down and rework Gallagher's story in collaboration with director Paul Joyce in order to turn it into a workable set of scripts:

> '[Steve Gallagher] really didn't know how to put a script together... [Paul Joyce and I] worked our way through this material, trying to be as true to what Steve was doing as

---

[18] Smith, Andrew, interview with author, 7 December 2017.
[19] Smith, interview with author.

possible, but at the same time making it a script with dialogue that actors could say.'[20]

The Keeper of Traken (1981) would present a very different problem, in that writer Johnny Byrne had gone on holiday after delivering his scripts and couldn't be contacted when Bidmead discovered that the scripts didn't meet his requirements: 'This was another script that wasn't right on the final delivery, though, and needed a lot of work. Johnny was unavailable to help me with it.'[21] This time, Bidmead alone carried out the necessary rewrite.

Starting with *Full Circle*, then, we have a run of four scripts that give Bidmead's authorial input at least as much weight as that of other scriptwriters and directors[22]. The relative inexperience of Andrew Smith and Stephen Gallagher as television writers and the absence of Johnny Byrne effectively gave Bidmead the opportunity to bring *Full Circle*, *Warriors' Gate* and *The Keeper of Traken* aesthetically into line with his own *Logopolis*, through suggestions to the writers and through his own rewrites.

---

[20] *Myth Makers* #87. Graeme Harper claims credit for writing the camera scripts based on Joyce's verbal instructions – see Spilsbury, Tom, 'Graeme Harper', DWM issue 380, p24 – but his input would have been purely technical and is unlikely to have affected the narrative.

[21] DWM Special Edition #16, p83. Or, as Bidmead less diplomatically puts it in *Myth Makers* #87, 'Johnny had decided that now was the time to go off for a holiday in Spain and he was completely incommunicado.'

[22] Although *Castrovalva* (1982) followed this run in transmission order, it fell in the middle of Season 19's production order and was the second script to be edited by Eric Saward. We might still think of it as a late outlier in a 'long Bidmead era'.

The Bidmead Masterplan

We can get a pretty good feel for the character of Bidmead's vision of **Doctor Who** by directly comparing *Full Circle* with the more traditional *State of Decay*. Both feature a society restrained in its development by three rulers, a terrible secret those rulers are keeping from the general population and an ancient spacecraft that nobody knows how to pilot. But where *State of Decay*'s Three Who Rule are malevolent and ultimately answer to a bigger, nastier intelligence, the Deciders are well-intentioned and aren't under the control of a higher authority. The Three Who Rule and the Great Vampire personally embody the horror of *State of Decay* and prey on their subjects; *Full Circle* finds horror in the impersonal natural processes that have made the Deciders as much victims as those they govern. The Doctor's victory in *State of Decay* involves defeating the individual threat of the vampires; the victory in *Full Circle* is a small, hopeful one against a broader existential problem.

Similarly in *The Keeper of Traken* and Bidmead's own *Logopolis*, while the pantomime villainy of the Master is foregrounded, the real peril in both stories comes from the natural decay of a once-stable environment – an impersonal natural process (in those cases, entropy) to which all the characters are subject. Whereas **Doctor Who** in the 1970s drew on melodramatic literature and film as an inspiration and a backdrop for its own tales of heroism, in Season 18 it draws on scientific principles (broadly expressed, perhaps) for inspiration and finds heroism in the struggle to understand and withstand natural laws. This shift in emphasis may be what Bidmead is thinking of when he speaks in interviews of trying to bring the science back to **Doctor Who** – giving the show a scientific ethos rather than literally foregrounding hard science[23]. In his interview for the fan-produced documentary series *Myth Makers*, Bidmead talks more specifically about trying to put the scientific method at the heart of the show, giving the Doctor a spirit of rational enquiry and getting him to solve problems through observation and hypothesis rather than by using his sonic screwdriver or K-9. Nowhere in Season 18 can this more clearly be seen than in the scenes of the Doctor uncovering the Deciders' terrible secret with a microscope in episode 4 of *Full Circle*.

Reformatting

The three stories that form the central portion of Season 18 – *Full Circle*, *State of Decay* and *Warriors' Gate* – are often referred to as the 'E-Space Trilogy'[24], which implies, rightly or wrongly, that they form a single larger story with a narrative arc running through it. Bidmead had first suggested 'a trilogy of stories with a linking theme' to John Nathan-Turner early in 1980 and finally codified his linking concept of E-Space in a document dated 12 June[25]. By that time, filming had already been completed on *State of Decay*.

---

[23] See, for example, Bidmead in conversation at the start of the DVD extra 'E-Space: Fact or Fiction?': 'I think I was specifically hired to bring a scientific sense back into **Doctor Who**.' As we'll see in Chapters 2 and 4, he wasn't entirely successful at putting nuts-and-bolts science into **Doctor Who**.

[24] See, most obviously, the packaging of the VHS and DVD releases of the three stories, which were released on both occasions in a single box under that umbrella title.

[25] Pixley, 'DWM Archive: Full Circle'.

Although Bidmead's linking theme would be worked into the three scripts of the trilogy, it would have relatively little impact on them.

Doctor Who had previously attempted arc storytelling in Season 16, in which the Doctor and Romana are given a mission to collect the scattered parts of the Key to Time and return them to the White Guardian. This is clearly a different case from the three E-Space stories, in which the backdrop of E-Space is a common feature but not a significant plot element. While the six stories of Season 16 clearly work as separate units, the quest for the Key to Time is foregrounded within them. Discovering the identity of each fragment of the Key and recovering it forms a central part of all stories except for the two scripted by David Fisher, *The Stones of Blood* and *The Androids of Tara* (both 1978), and even so in the latter his early sidelining of the quest for the Key is done in order to make a point about the protagonists' personalities and to move them into position for his own story. More to the point, the concept of the Key to Time as a driving element of the overall season was worked out well in advance[26], and far from being grafted onto a set of pre-existing scripts as in the case of E-Space, it was incorporated into the stories of Season 16 at the commissioning stage.

By contrast, connectivity between stories in **Doctor Who** in the 1980s tends to be created through 'continuity references' that relate current stories to earlier ones, or through less tangible thematic elements carried across from one story to another. Fans often disparage this tendency in 80s **Who** as 'soap opera', but that

---

[26] As early as November 1976, in fact, when a detailed pitch of the season-spanning concept formed part of Graham Williams' application for the position of producer. See *In-Vision* #38, p2-3.

would imply a greater degree of connectivity between episodes than was attempted in **Doctor Who** at this time. There's a less centralised feel to 80s **Who**; rather than a preconceived overarching story, we have an assortment of unrelated stories that the script editor has attempted to fit together – thematically, narratively or on both levels – by introducing common elements at a later stage of script development.

This loosely connective approach, as well as the decision to expand the number of the Doctor's companions to three over the course of Season 18, might suggest to us that Bidmead and Nathan-Turner were attempting to emulate the format of **Doctor Who** in the 1960s, but it isn't quite that either. **Who** stories in the 60s would routinely end with a teaser scene that set up the story that followed, much in the manner of the cinematic adventure serials of earlier decades; this was down to the story editor (as the position was then known) adding linking elements to otherwise unrelated stories in order to create the feel of a continuing adventure across stories. Yet direct links between stories in this vein were made only infrequently in the 80s, most commonly during the period 1982-84, when Peter Davison was in the title role, and then only rarely using the cliffhanger format that had joined stories together in the 60s.

Instances of this in Seasons 19 to 21 include: Nyssa's collapse at the end of *Four to Doomsday* (1982) setting up her absence from *Kinda* (1982); *Time-Flight* (1982) dealing briefly and half-heartedly with Adric's death in *Earthshock* (1982); the TARDIS being pulled off course at the end of *Frontios* (1984) into what is revealed to be a time corridor at the start of *Resurrection of the Daleks* (1984); and the unavoidable carry-over of the regeneration from *The Caves of Androzani* (1984) into *The Twin Dilemma* (1984)[27]. There's also the 'Black Guardian Trilogy' of Season 20[28], which is more cohesive overall and makes more prominent use of its arc elements than the 'E-Space Trilogy'.

In Season 18, this type of connectivity between stories is very rare, with only the summons from Gallifrey at the end of *Meglos* and the Master's triumph at the end of *The Keeper of Traken* carrying over directly from one story into the next; the TARDIS' return to normal space at the end of *Warriors' Gate* is picked up on in the first moments of *The Keeper of Traken*, but there's no real carry-over of story content. The 'E-Space Trilogy' itself shows its roots as three unrelated stories rather than as a single planned sequence – the concept of E-Space barely impacts on *Full Circle* or on *State of Decay*, and while it presumably didn't take much wrangling to turn the surreal 'dream time' of Steve Gallagher's original story submission[29] into the gateway/pocket universe of *Warriors' Gate*, that story refers only glancingly to E-Space and might as easily have played out on its own in another season. The arc of the perceived trilogy is formed by secondary elements that have been grafted onto these otherwise standalone stories.

---

[27] Tegan's departure in *Time-Flight* and return in *Arc of Infinity* (1983), falling across seasons, probably doesn't belong in this list. We might perhaps view it as a precursor of the trans-season arcs of Matt Smith's tenure.

[28] Consisting of *Mawdryn Undead*, *Terminus* and *Enlightenment* (all 1983).

[29] *In-Vision* #50, p5.

These elements are only really resolved in *Logopolis*, when the origin of the 'charged vacuum emboitement' (CVE) that gives access to E-space is revealed as part of the Logopolitans' efforts to prevent the collapse of the universe. Together with the Master's return in *The Keeper of Traken* and the foreshadowing in that story of *Logopolis* – natural entropy held at bay by something half-science and half-magic that the Master tries and fails to control – the narrative thread of the CVE forms part of a looser thematic arc that encompasses not three stories but five.

This approach to long-form storytelling in TV shows comprised of shorter stories is familiar to us in the 'season arc' structure in common use today. Notable prior examples of arc storytelling of this type in British television include the fourth series (1969) of **Public Eye** (1965-75), which sees its hero – a down-at-heel private investigator – gradually recovering his life and career after a year of wrongful imprisonment; and a number of storylines in secret service thriller **Callan** (1967-72), culminating in a trio of episodes that pit Callan against his Soviet opposite number. Although a successful and widely-used device in British television generally, the 'season arc' is a rarity in **Doctor Who** during the 20th century; Season 8 (1971), with its sustained focus on the newly introduced character of the Master, could also arguably be considered an example of the form. Since 2005, however, it has become a routine feature of the show.

In these cases the season comprises a mixture of stories that are essentially standalone, linked by background and thematic elements, and episodes that exist largely or entirely to serve the arc story. The clearest example of this in 21st-century **Doctor Who** is probably the 2005 series, in which the setting of Satellite Five, mid-series companion Captain Jack Harkness, Margaret Blaine's extrapolator and concepts such as Dalek-human hybridisation and opening the TARDIS console to access the power within it are seeded across the season[30] and then drawn together in the final episodes, *Bad Wolf* and *The Parting of the Ways* (both 2005), along with an explanation of the recurring phrase 'Bad Wolf'. Season 18 is much closer to this format than it is to the more straightforwardly-planned format of Season 16.

All Change

Full Circle also marks the start of John Nathan-Turner's overhaul of **Doctor Who**'s regular cast. By the end of Season 18 all the leads would be replaced and the show would have a new Doctor, three new companions and the return of the Master as a recurring villain. That process begins here with the introduction of Adric; moreover, it's *Full Circle* which signals the imminent departure of the old companions. Romana's response in episode 1 to the order to return to Gallifrey sets up a clear expectation that, either by obeying or evading the summons, she'll be leaving the TARDIS soon; her story threatens to come full circle. A line of dialogue from the Doctor reminds older viewers and informs newer ones that the Doctor's previous companions – Leela and the original K-9 – had been left on Gallifrey, and those viewers might have expected a similar send-off for Romana and K-9 Mark Two. As it turns out, both will remain in E-Space at the end of the trio of stories that starts with *Full Circle*.

---

[30] In *The Long Game, The Empty Child, Boom Town, Dalek* and *Boom Town* again respectively (all 2005).

Notions of circularity are echoed elsewhere in Season 18, notably in the concept of recursion that Bidmead briefly explores in *Logopolis* and will revisit in *Castrovalva* (1982). We get a foretaste of this concept in *Full Circle*, although it isn't identified as such in the script, in the form of the Starliner. The Starliner is a foreign space within the world of Alzarius, an environment in itself that occupies the wider environment of the planet. Alzarius in its turn occupies the environment of the Starliner through the form of the Marshmen. There are definite echoes of this, conceptually if not narratively or visually, in the mutual occupation of the Doctor's and Master's TARDISes in *Logopolis*.

The cyclical nature of **Doctor Who** itself as an episodic series is reinforced at the end of *Full Circle*. At the conclusion of the story, as at the start, we see the Doctor, Romana and K-9 at liberty to explore the universe together; it's a different universe, but the fact that they've been relocated to E-Space seems as much an opportunity for adventure and discovery as a problem to be solved. It's almost a wiping of the slate for the show, a new universe and a fresh start, even though at the same time it's a reaffirmation of the status quo that was threatened by Romana's summons to return to Gallifrey in episode 1 and by K-9's apparent destruction in episode 2.

CHAPTER 2: HOPEFUL MONSTERS

Although *Full Circle* is ostensibly a story about evolution, or at least a story that seems to explore the concept, its grasp of the subject is a bit shaky. The prevailing concept of evolutionary theory at the time the programme was made, and probably still the one most readers will share, is one based on Charles Darwin's publications of the 19th century and refined in the light of advances in genetic research in the early 20th century – that species change and diversify in response to environmental pressures, through the process of natural selection. Individuals whose small-scale genetic mutations give them an advantage are able to survive and breed, while individuals whose mutations put them at a disadvantage are killed or otherwise prevented from reproducing, and over the course of multiple generations these tiny, incremental adaptations add up to significant changes in the species. What we see in *Full Circle* is a world in which a collection of life forms, indistinguishable at the cellular level, evolves very rapidly through a combination of learned experience and exposure to new environments, and apparently not in response to environmental pressures but deliberately by their own will to imitate and replace other life forms.

Although the natural history of life on Alzarius bears little relation to commonly accepted evolutionary theory, it does – albeit without any intent on the part of Andrew Smith or Christopher H Bidmead – illustrate a few related ideas, alternative hypotheses of species development that were once popular but have since been discredited. It's closer to the scientific consensus of the 1900s than of the 1980s – arguably appropriate, given the Doctor's fondness for Edwardian fashion and the show's roots in Wellsian science fiction.

One such discredited hypothesis is Ernst Haeckel's Biogenetic Law, formulated in 1866, which he summed up with the phrase 'Ontogeny recapitulates phylogeny'[31]. In plain English, what Haeckel was suggesting was that the stages of physical development a gestating embryo goes through (ontogeny) are a reflection of the earlier physical forms of its species (phylogeny). *Full Circle* could perhaps be said to recapitulate the phylogeny of evolutionary theory itself[32].

(Note: I'll mostly use the word 'Alzarians' throughout this book as a way of distinguishing the later inhabitants of the Starliner, the human-like characters depicted in *Full Circle*, from the original inhabitants of the Starliner, the Terradonians that we never see. However, in this chapter I'll use it slightly differently, as a convenient way of referring generally to native life forms that have 'evolved' to mimic the original Terradonians – not just the Alzarians the Doctor meets in this story, but any potential earlier or later generations of former Marshmen who might undergo the same mutation.)

Spontaneous Generation

The circle of life on Alzarius begins with the riverfruit, which the Alzarians are seen harvesting in readiness for Mistfall at the start of

---

[31] Haeckel, Ernst, *Generelle Morphologie der Organismen* (1866). See also Gould, Stephen Jay, *Ontogeny and Phylogeny* (1977).
[32] Which would tie in nicely with the theme of recursion as explored in Bidmead's *Logopolis* and *Castrovalva*.

the story. What appear to be pips inside the riverfruit later prove to be the beginnings of the marsh spiders – Dexeter suggests to Draith in episode 1 that they might be 'eggs of some kind', although he's only repeating the speculation of an earlier generation. His further comment that 'unfamiliar insect life is supposed to precede each incident' suggests that his predecessors didn't study the spiders in any great depth[33]. Are the 'eggs' pips after all? Were they laid inside the riverfruit by an unobserved variety of 'unfamiliar insect life', or did they form inside the fruit?

This ambiguous scene, and the later scenes of the spiders bursting out of the ripe fruit, are reminiscent of the theory of spontaneous generation, which was once a widely accepted explanation of where pest animals such as flies and rats came from. The theory ran that these 'lower' forms of life would form spontaneously under the right conditions, usually in dead or inanimate matter, and it can be traced back at least as far as the ancient Greeks. Aristotle wasn't the first to write down his thoughts on this subject, but he went into more detail than his predecessors, stating in the fifth book of his *History of Animals* that some animals 'come from putrefying earth or vegetable matter' while others might be born out of mud or snow[34]. St Augustine of Hippo popularised Aristotle's theory among Christians in the fourth and fifth centuries, suggesting in a commentary on the Old Testament book of *Genesis* that 'certain very small animals [...] may have originated later from putrefying

---

[33] It also gives a mystical, folkloric air to his supposedly scientific inquiry, which Draith's doomy rumblings about the System Files only reinforce. See also Chapter 4.
[34] Aristotle, *A History of Animals*, p100.

matter'[35]. Such beliefs were popularly held in the Western world well into the 19th century, and were only laid to rest by Louis Pasteur's research into microbial life, for which he was awarded a prize of 2,500 francs by the French Academy of Sciences in 1862[36].

The appearance of the Marshmen at the end of episode 1 is every bit as spontaneous as that of the spiders at the end of episode 2; it's also suggestive of the amphibious origins of land-based species including our own ancestors, or of the earlier emergence of life itself from a primordial liquid. This idea, of a rich slime acting as the source of living things on a previously lifeless planet, also has its roots in Greek philosophy, with the idea that life first emerged from the sea or was created by the congealment of land from water[37]. A more scientific version of this concept was put forward by Lorenz Oken who suggested that life on Earth might have arisen from a kind of cellular protoplasm or 'Urschleim'[38]. In 1924, Alexander Oparin suggested that Earth in its geological infancy could have had an atmosphere like that of the gas giants, rich in methane and

---

[35] White, Andrew Dickson, *A History of the Warfare of Science with Theology in Christendom* (1922), p53.

[36] A counterpoint to the notion of spontaneous generation was the now equally outdated doctrine of preformation, which supposed that all future generations of a given life form were pre-packaged in that life form's gonads, one inside another like a microscopic set of Russian dolls. This concept was popularized by the 18th century Genevan naturalist Charles Bonnet in a 1762 work titled *Considérations sur les corps organisés*. His word for it? 'Emboîtement'.

[37] Osborn, Henry Fairfield, *From the Greeks to Darwin: An Outline of the Development of the Evolution Idea* (1905), p33-36.

[38] Magner, Lois N, *A History of the Life Sciences* (2002), p152.

ammonia, and that in such an environment simple organic compounds could have organised themselves into more complex forms[39]. It wasn't until 1953 that Stanley Miller published an account of the experiment he and Harold Urey had carried out that recreated a 'primordial soup' in the laboratory under the conditions Oparin had suggested[40]. The scenes of the Alzarian marsh shrouded in mist are suggestive of this primordial environment.

Evolutionary Theory – Darwin and Lamarck

Like life on Earth, the native life forms of Alzarius – the spiders, the Marshmen and the Alzarians – derive from a single biochemical source, as revealed by their identical cellular structure and the Doctor's investigation of their shared genetic heritage. The horror of the Deciders at this revelation equally clearly evokes the horror of Victorian society at the writings of Charles Darwin and other contemporary natural historians. Darwin was the first to make an explicit evolutionary connection between humans and other terrestrial animals, hinting at it in *On the Origin of Species* in 1859 and fully detailing it in *The Descent of Man* in 1871. Prior to that, scientists and theologians (and both terms could often be applied to the same person) had generally agreed that humans were not related to other animals, either because the process of evolution had started after the Biblical creation or because humans had been specially created by God. By not exempting humans in this way and treating them as subject to the same natural processes as other living things, Darwin encouraged an exclusively scientific approach

---

[39] Oparin, AI, *The Origin of Life* (1953).
[40] Miller, Stanley L, 'Production of Amino Acids Under Possible Primitive Earth Conditions'.

to natural history and so effectively upended the relationship between science and religion in the 19th century. It isn't too fanciful to see the Doctor performing a similar role in *Full Circle*, overturning the regime of the Deciders – stuck in their ways, treating secular truths as holy mysteries and keeping the people in their care occupied with ritual activity – by giving the Alzarians scientific mastery of the Starliner.

Despite his profound influence on the Western scientific community, the fine detail of Darwin's hypothesis – that species are gradually changed through natural selection – was neglected for several decades. It wasn't until the discovery of genetics in the 1930s that scientists started to take Darwin's concept of natural selection seriously as a mechanism for evolutionary change.

During the intervening decades, probably the biggest influence on evolutionary thought was Jean-Baptiste Lamarck's work *Zoological Philosophy*, first published in 1809. Two ideas in particular influenced the scientists of the late 19th and early 20th centuries, although neither was original to Lamarck. One of these was the suggestion that physiological changes undergone during an individual's lifetime would be inherited by that individual's offspring – that, for example, a creature that strongly exercised one particular muscle during its formative years would give birth to creatures in which that muscle was more highly developed. This hypothesis, as codified by Lamarck, was based on the writings of Darwin's grandfather Erasmus Darwin[41]. The other was the notion of evolution as a teleological process, a meaningful one-way progression from simpler forms to increasingly complex ones. Later

---

[41] Darwin, Erasmus, *Zoonomia: Or, the Laws of Organic Life* (1796).

scientists such as Wilhelm Haacke and Theodor Eimer developed from this the concept of orthogenesis, the idea that evolution is directed from within the organism by some innate blueprint rather than by external factors. But the idea has its roots in the much older belief in a 'chain of being', a natural hierarchy with human beings at the top as the most perfect living thing. The 'chain of being', like spontaneous generation, was an idea taken from Aristotle's *History of Animals* and popularised by Augustine of Hippo, and would have resonated with early Christians' belief in humanity's supremacy over other, less complex and therefore less godly animals.

Both of these ideas can be seen in action in *Full Circle*, which owes much more to the Lamarckian concept of evolution than it does to the Darwinian concept. We see the Marshmen emerge for the first time from underwater and almost immediately acclimatise to the atmosphere away from the marsh and to the air inside the Starliner, and as we're told that this is how the Alzarians' ancestors started out, it's reasonable to assume that this physiological change will be passed on to a new, mutated generation of Marshmen born on dry land. That they adapt so quickly – even purposefully – to the oxygenated air rather than staying in the water underscores the sense that their development has a direction and a goal, to change from the shambling, smooth-featured creatures we first see to copies of the physically and socially complex Alzarians. Moreover, the fact that the Alzarians' ancestors evolved in this exact way, apparently through their own will to enter the Starliner and replace its occupants, tells us that evolution on Alzarius is a repeatable, delineated process with a definite goal in mind.

Saltation

Another idea that was popular during the late 19th and early 20th centuries was saltation (literally, 'jumping') – the idea that, contrary to the notion of gradual generational change put forward by both Darwin and Lamarck, evolution might be driven by large, sudden mutations. Rather than species slowly evolving to fit into an environmental niche, according to the hypothesis of saltation individuals within a species might undergo physical mutations that would cripple them in their original habitat, but would allow them to survive in an environment that was more hospitable to those mutations, provided such an environment existed. Successful mutants might then breed and occupy their new environment, effectively becoming a new species. Quantum leaps in the development of life on Earth, such as the amphibious movement from sea to land or the growth of gripping limbs, were seen as evidence in favour of this theory. Richard Goldschmidt, revisiting the hypothesis of saltation in 1940, coined the term 'hopeful monster' to describe these mutants in search of a welcoming habitat[42]. Writing after the concept of saltationary evolution had been rejected in favour of Darwinian natural selection, Goldschmidt was mocked by his peers, but scientists have since speculated that evolution in practice might require some combination of saltation and natural selection, of large changes and fine tuning. Discoveries in the field of genetics have shown that small mutations in a single gene during the early development of an organism can cause significant changes to its mature physical structure, which suggests

---

[42] Goldschmidt, Richard, *The Material Basis of Evolution* (1940), p390.

that the notion of saltationary evolution might be more plausible than it first seems[43].

The hypothesis of saltation might help us to make sense of the evolutionary process on Alzarius. Even allowing for the unusual rapidity of biological growth and change, it's strange that the development of animal life on Alzarius should run from spiders to Marshmen to Alzarians with no visible interim stages. Presumably the birds that the Doctor disturbs in episode 1 also fit into that sequence somewhere, although that doesn't exactly help to clear things up. But in practice, what we're shown is a hyperadaptive life form that leaps unerringly from a form suited to hatching out of riverfruit to one suited to amphibious life, to one suited to operating a Terradonian Starliner. Alzarius offers an entire biosphere of successful 'hopeful monsters'.

A Specious Origin

As a primer on the theory of evolution by natural selection, *Full Circle* is a non-starter. In fact, the best illustration of real-world biology comes not from anything in the story itself but through the metaphor of the Starliner. The genetic code that it carries – the instruction manuals in the Great Book Room – gives its Alzarian cells the instructions necessary to perform basic maintenance and keep the ship ticking over, but no details of how to take off or where to go, no teleological information.

---

[43] See, for example, Gould, SJ, 'Return of the Hopeful Monster', or Dawkins, Richard, *Climbing Mount Improbable* (1996). The Doctor seems to favour the hypothesis too, observing in episode 4 that 'evolution goes in quantum leaps'. (He further notes that 'it doesn't go **that** fast', but on Alzarius it appears that it does.)

But it would be wrong to imagine that the point of the story is to teach us about evolution, and *Full Circle* is far from the only story to play fast and loose with the concept of evolution for entertainment's sake. In the **Star Trek: The Next Generation** episode *Genesis* (1994), the reactivation of dormant genes causes one human crewmember to 'devolve' into a gigantic spider. The whole concept of 'devolving' – the idea that evolution is a mechanism, intrinsic to the organism and independent of environment, that can be thrown into reverse – is tied in with the discredited theory of evolution by orthogenesis as previously described. **Doctor Who** trod similar ground in *The Lazarus Experiment* (2007), with its suggestion that human beings are just one bad science experiment away from mutating into vampiric scorpion monsters. Science fiction on TV and in print is littered with other examples of human characters evolving or mutating in ways that defy real-world genetic and evolutionary theories, as well as the ever-popular notion that evolution is a teleological process, a linear track that can be travelled backward ('devolution') or forward, usually with human beings destined to become creatures of pure intelligence.

The hints of evolutionary concepts in *Full Circle* really only give a cover of 'scienciness' to a story that in many ways borders on the realms of parascience and mysticism. They're of a piece with the presentation of the Source in *The Keeper of Traken* as a bit of machinery, or the description of entropy as something that can be localised and siphoned out of the universe in *Logopolis*. This aspect of *Full Circle* will be examined in more detail in Chapter 4.

Doctor Who likes to ramp up the significance of its monsters or villains by stating that they've directed the development of human

38

civilisation to their own benefit; Azal, Scaroth and the Silence are stand-out examples of this[44]. *Image of the Fendahl* (1977) one-ups this by suggesting that the entire course of human evolution has been perverted by the Fendahl, while evolution itself becomes a source of horror in *Ghost Light* (1989)[45]. *Full Circle* sits alongside *Image of the Fendahl* as a story in which evolution has been directed in a way that undermines the protagonists' concept of their history and themselves, but with the important difference that no external agency is involved.

Like *Ghost Light* it presents hyperevolutionary beings as a source of threat and spectacle, but with the twist that they and the beings they are in conflict with are related and motivated only by their shared biology. Evolution, or at least the unusual system of mutation and mimicry that passes for evolution on Alzarius, is itself responsible for steering Alzarian life towards a predetermined end result. This is the terrible secret that the Deciders keep and the Doctor uncovers. No sinister guiding hand is revealed; the teleology of life on Alzarius, while apparently deliberate, doesn't serve any ulterior purpose. It appears to be a reflexive action on the part of the planetary ecosystem in response to the Starliner's original

---

[44] *The Dæmons* (1971), *City of Death* (1979) and *The Impossible Astronaut / Day of the Moon* (2011) respectively.
[45] It's surprising that more **Doctor Who** stories haven't gone down this route. For a science-fiction series that wants to tell Gothic stories (or 'post-Gothic' stories; see Bucher-Jones, *The Black Archive #5: Image of the Fendahl*) – stories whose protagonists are affected in a disturbing way by the actions of their ancestors – evolution ought to be an indispensable prop.

crash, the Starliner imprinting itself on the planet in more than just the literal sense.

Which begs the question: is Alzarius itself a living organism?

CHAPTER 3: A NEW LOOK AT LIFE ON ALZARIUS

In 1979, Dr James Lovelock published a pop science book called *Gaia: A New Look at Life on Earth*. This book was built around his hypothesis that all living things on Earth and the inorganic environment that supports them work together to form a single self-regulating system – that, ever since the physical conditions on Earth allowed life to develop in the first place, the chemical interactions of all life forms and their surroundings have held those physical conditions within the narrow parameters necessary to continue to support life. Lovelock wasn't suggesting that the entire planet, rocks and all, was actually a single organism, only that its biochemical processes could be understood in similar terms to those of the organism. Nonetheless, his book has sometimes been misinterpreted along those lines[46], and it's easy to see why.

Lovelock used the name 'Gaia'[47] to refer to this system of chemical feedback loops, partly because it had all of the convenience and none of the ugliness of an acronym, and partly to make the idea more relatable for his readers. The downside of this is that the reader might too easily suppose Lovelock was depicting the Earth itself as an intelligent being, personifying it by naming it in this way.

---

[46] See, for example, Troy Kennedy Martin discussing his inspiration for writing the BBC thriller series **Edge of Darkness** (1985) in the DVD extra 'Magnox – The Secrets of **Edge of Darkness**'.

[47] The name of an ancient Greek goddess personifying the Earth; as Lovelock admits in his opening chapter, the name was suggested to him by his neighbour William Golding (Lovelock, James, *Gaia: A New Look at Life on Earth* p10).

In his preface to the 2000 edition of the book, Lovelock insists that he was simply exercising poetic licence for the benefit of his non-scientist readers, but not all of his readers drew a distinction between the poetry and the science. In the decades that followed its publication, *Gaia* was scorned by the orthodox scientific community and hailed as a visionary text by the New Age contingent of the environmental movement.

'Living planets' In prose science fiction tend not to be planets that are themselves intelligent, communicative organisms, but more usually superorganisms wherein all the parts of a planet's biosphere work as one entity, like a planet-scale coral reef or insect hive. This is only one small twist of poetic licence away from Lovelock's notion of a planet-scale homeostatic system. The stand-out example of a planetary superorganism in science fiction, and the only significant example pre-1980, is the sentient ocean in Stanislaw Lem's *Solaris* (1961), filmed in 1972 by Andrei Tarkovsky. A couple of years after the publication of *Gaia*, Isaac Asimov would use the same name for a man-made superorganism in his novel *Foundation's Edge* (1982).

Planets that are capable of holding a conversation with human characters are hard to find outside the world of comic books. The only example of a thinking, speaking planet that predates *Full Circle* is Ego the Living Planet, created by Jack Kirby for Marvel Cumlcs[48]. Ego is villainous and has a literal gigantic face, in print at least; in his only film appearance to date he was portrayed as a brain with a planet-like casing and a human-sized avatar played by Kurt Russell[49]. DC Comics produced their own take in 1985, Mogo the

---

[48] Lee, Stan, et al, 'Rigel – Where Gods May Fear to Tread!'
[49] *Guardians of the Galaxy Vol. 2* (2017).

Living Planet, which is heroic and doesn't have a face, although it is a paid-up member of the Green Lantern Corps[50].

The chief precedents for 'living planets' in **Doctor Who** in 1980 were a joking reference to Magla, 'an 8,000 mile wide amoeba that's grown a crusty shell'[51], and the implication that the primordial sludge dredged up by the Stahlman Project represents some animate property of our own Earth[52]. More recently we've seen a sentient gas giant, an apparently sentient star, a highly articulate evil asteroid and the revelation that Earth's Moon is the egg of an alien organism[53], suggesting that **Doctor Who** is more open to depicting the more fantastic forms of 'living planet' today than it was in the 1980s[54].

At the time *Full Circle* was being written, *Gaia* would have been a hot topic of conversation – Bidmead, an avid reader of *New Scientist*, would certainly have heard the details even if he hadn't then read the book. And yet *Gaia* apparently exerted no direct influence on the story, and little if any indirect influence through Bidmead. Smith has never read Lovelock's work and can't recall it being mentioned at any of his meetings with Bidmead, but insists

---

[50] Moore, Alan, et al, 'Tales of the Green Lantern Corps: Mogo Doesn't Socialize'.
[51] *Destiny of the Daleks* (1979), episode 1.
[52] *Inferno* (1970).
[53] *The Rings of Akhaten* (2013), *42* (2007), *The Doctor's Wife* (2011), and *Kill the Moon* (2014) respectively.
[54] *In the Forest of the Night* (2014) further suggests that Earth's trees are intelligent and capable of working as a single superorganism, which may or may not hint at the Earth itself being sentient.

that the very Gaian concept of a 'living planet' was central to the story right from the start, as reflected in his original title, 'The Planet That Slept':

> 'The very core of the idea was the planet [...] It is all kind of interconnected and the idea was that it's a living thing, not like a sentient planet, but it is a living thing [...] I did kind of think of the Marshmen as being the offspring of the planet, as are the spiders and everything else, and all connected by the same DNA.'[55]

This is broadly hinted at in *Full Circle* and its novelisation. Smith has since taken the opportunity to expand on the idea in *Mistfall* (2015), a Big Finish audio sequel to *Full Circle*:

> 'In the *Mistfall* CD that's clarified in that it is shown that everything is connected; I don't want to call it a power source, but there's a crystalline source that sort of permeates the soil and the water and everything and provides this interconnection between all the fauna on Alzarius.'[56]

Despite Smith's assertion that Alzarius wasn't meant to be sentient in its own right, there's more than a hint in *Full Circle* that the creatures of Alzarius are connected not just by biology but by a form of consciousness. Romana's behaviour in episodes 3 and 4 provides the strongest evidence for this. The venom of the spider

---

[55] Smith, interview with author.

[56] Smith, interview with author. If only the Doctor had compared a soil sample with those tissue samples from Dexeter, the Marshchild and the spider!

that bites her puts her into a kind of trance in which she seems to share a telepathic connection with the Marshmen; she screams at the same moment that Dexeter begins his vivisection of the Marshchild; and she acts in concert with the Marshmen outside the Starliner when she opens the door to let them in. It's as if the planet Alzarius uses the Marshmen as its tools and orchestrates them through the medium of the psychochemical spider venom.

Later in episode 4, we see that those Alzarians killed by the Marshmen show the same glowing veins on their face as Romana, implying that the Marshmen can also pass the venom on to others – the Doctor appears concerned that the Alzarians should avoid even touching the Marshmen, so possibly in their case the psychochemical is transmitted through the skin rather than by biting. But we never see any Alzarians communing with the Marshmen in the way that Romana does. There are no scenes of living Alzarians with glowing veins, only dead ones. We might initially suppose while watching episode 4 that the Marshmen have killed their victims through physical violence, but it could rather be that the Alzarians have diverged so far biologically from the Marshmen that the psychochemical that connects them, and that is strong enough to overwhelm Romana's Gallifreyan physiology, is now lethal to them[57].

---

[57] The spiders might be a danger to the Marshmen in much the same way, judging from their behaviour at the end of episode 2 – perhaps the key difference between the Marshmen and the Alzarians is that the former are still sufficiently connected to the biosphere that they know to keep their distance. Then again, they all seem to be looking at the TARDIS rather than in the direction of the spiders as they back out of the cave. Perhaps Romana's wrong

Has the evolution of the Alzarians from Marshmen to imitation Terradonians split them off from the planetary organism? This certainly would be in line with Smith's intentions:

> 'Alzarius is their home but it's a home that they don't fit into, they've evolved beyond it. The funny thing is, thinking about it now, they've evolved beyond it but the planet hasn't.'[58]

Towards the end of his novelisation, Smith presents a scene from the point of view of the Marshmen, 'the guardians of Alzarius' whose chosen purpose is 'to serve and to protect nature on this planet', as they consider the problem of 'the non-people' who 'had discarded this philosophy and allowed the corruption of off-world to infect them'[59]. There's an uncomfortable edge to this vision of a community that considers its peers to be so corrupted by outside influences that it no longer regards them as people – the physical mutation of the Alzarians recast as a political or ideological change violently rejected by an 'uncorrupted' old guard. It would be tempting but facile to inflate this bit of paratextual detail into a kind of socio-political commentary. It would be even easier to take the point that both sides are really the same underneath it all as a simplistic commentary on racism. But surely *Full Circle* has something more interesting, something weirder to say than this?

Perhaps we should think of the original Terradonians as microbial invaders in the body of the living planet Alzarius. The Marshmen killed them – acting as antibodies? – but were unable to remove the foreign body of the Starliner and were themselves subverted by

---

when she speculates that they've been scared off by the spiders.
[58] Smith, interview with author.
[59] Smith, Andrew, *Doctor Who: Full Circle*, p62.

it. The physical template and even the knowledge of the Terradonians has somehow infected them, and as a result they've become foreign organisms themselves – a sort of planetary lymphatic cancer. In fact, they've done rather better than the Terradonians – presumably thanks to their own hyperadaptability – in holding back subsequent waves of apparently murderous Marshmen[60]. In this reading of the story, the Doctor doesn't so much help the Alzarians by showing them how to leave the planet, as help Alzarius by enabling it to eject the Starliner from its biosphere. The desire of the Marshmen to drive out the Alzarians and the desire of the Alzarians to fix the Starliner and leave could be the same impulse – to get the Terradonians off the surface of the planet – carried across from one biological form to another.

---

[60] Or have they? Perhaps there were several rounds of Marshmen killing off their predecessors and fending off their successors, each time with more success, culminating in the population of Alzarians we see in this story.

CHAPTER 4: THE MAGIC (FULL) CIRCLE

As we saw in Chapter 1, Christopher H Bidmead started working on **Doctor Who** with the intention of injecting more scientific content into the show, or at least of having the Doctor approach problems in a scientific way. And yet it's striking that, for all that scientific concepts and a spirit of scientific inquiry are brought to the fore in Season 18, the stories in this season are framed in a way that often borders on the mystical.

We might think first of the science wizards of Traken or Logopolis; Clarke's Third Law says that any sufficiently advanced technology is indistinguishable from magic[61], and this seems to be the law of the land on those worlds. The Tachyon Recreation Generator in *The Leisure Hive* and the Dodecahedron in *Meglos* are capable of almost magical feats beyond anything we might reasonably expect of them, and the dimensional forces at work in *Warriors' Gate*, while presumably scientific, are certainly baffling to the characters and the viewer; but these are more or less in line with the treatment of science in the bulk of mainstream science fiction. At the other end of the scale, in *Full Circle* and *State of Decay* we have science that is poorly understood, science that might as well be magic to the people living alongside it, in the form of the Starliner and the Hydrax.

_____

[61] Science fiction writer Arthur C Clarke listed his three laws – in the style of Murphy's Law, a set of smart-alecky observations – in a 1973 essay (in *Profiles of the Future*, revised ed). **Doctor Who** fans may be more familiar with the quoting and adaptation of Clarke's Third Law in a deleted scene from *Battlefield* (1989).

State of Decay goes one step further towards the mystical by including vampires as its villains, and there's no attempt within the story to present them as anything other than supernatural[62]. But it's *Full Circle* that does the most in Season 18 to subvert Bidmead's supposed scientific vision for the series, flirting openly with the imagery of magic and undermining the credibility of scientists and technology throughout its four episodes.

Through the Looking Glass

The original character outline for Adric, composed by Bidmead and John Nathan-Turner, has him originating 'on a planet we'll call Yerfillag'[63]. Anagrams are a bit of a feature of 80s **Who**, usually frivolous (see, for example, the increasingly tortuous efforts to disguise the appearance of the Master in the *Radio Times* listings), but sometimes offering a hint at the nature of a character or the writer's thought processes. The Foamasi in *The Leisure Hive* get their name from an anagram of 'mafiosa', for example, because it was originally writer David Fisher's intention that the villains of his story should be portrayed as mafia-style thugs. Giving the draft version of Adric's planet a name that's blatantly 'Gallifrey' spelled

---

[62] *In-Vision* #49 notes Bidmead's suggestion at the scripting stage that the Three Who Rule, 'far from being vampires in the mythical sense, were only in this state because they had become possessed by the mental exertions of a tremendously powerful bat-like alien' (p4). This still leaves the Great Vampire as a near enough supernatural force in the story, and hardly rationalises the vampiric nature of the Three. In any case, the detail was lost in the transmitted programme.

[63] Howe, David J, and Mark Stammers, *Doctor Who: Companions*, p89.

backwards, added to the fact that it occupies the negative equivalent of Gallifrey's co-ordinates, suggests that it might have been the production team's intention that the two worlds – and by extension, perhaps Adric and the Doctor – should mirror each other to a greater extent than they do in the final scripts.

Andrew Smith rejects this supposition, stating that the suggestive name was 'always a placeholder':

> 'Alzarius is in the E-Space equivalent of the co-ordinates of Gallifrey, and that's why it was called 'Yerfillag', but there was never an intention, there was never a second's discussion about Alzarius being in any way, shape or form a version of Gallifrey, or that Adric was going to be like a younger version of the Doctor, or anything like that.'[64]

Intentionally or not, there are some interesting points of comparison between the respective societies of Gallifrey and Alzarius. As a fan of **Doctor Who** since the Troughton era, Smith would certainly have been aware of the details of Time Lord society as depicted hitherto; it's a stretch, but it's just barely possible that, nudged by the sight of the name 'Yerfillag' in Adric's character outline, he might have subconsciously incorporated some echoes of those details into his depiction of Alzarian society in later drafts of the scripts.

The Gallifreyans have expanded their scientific knowledge to the point that they've mastered time travel – and they count the Doctor, that consummate scientist and debunker of the supernatural, among their number – but their control of time has

---

[64] Smith, interview with author.

given them godlike power, and their portrayal in their earliest on-screen appearances plays into this. In *The War Games* (1969) they come across as nothing less than omnipotent, implacable deities. They're knocked down a peg or two in *Colony in Space* (1971) and *The Three Doctors* (1973), but they still have an aloof and somewhat mystical air about them. *The Three Doctors* also introduces the character of Omega, one of the founders of Time Lord society, who is described in this and later stories as having made time travel possible by harnessing the power of a black hole in a feat of engineering, but who is shown living in a magical fantasy castle held together by the sheer power of his will and who openly fancies himself a god. Robert Holmes may have tried to undermine the mystique of the Time Lords by turning them into petty bureaucrats in *The Deadly Assassin* (1976), but the layers of ritual and formality he included in that story, coupled with the grandiose set design, perversely paint their society in even more religious or magical tones. A large part of Holmes' plot turns on the Doctor's discovery that the ceremonial trappings of the Presidency are actually ancient and extremely powerful pieces of technology. Gallifrey is a place where scientific artefacts are elevated to the status of holy relics, left behind by ancestors who are themselves presented as gods above the civilisation they created.

The Alzarians have similarly inherited technology that they don't understand and have built rituals around it, in their case the pointless running repairs of the Starliner and the ceremony with which the Deciders rule. Smith recalls Bidmead talking about the never-ending maintenance of the Starliner specifically in terms of ritual:

'I do remember when we were walking to the readthrough actually, Chris saying he had in mind that there'd be an element of the cargo cult [...] I think his idea there was it was ritual without really knowing what was behind the ritual.'[65]

There are also definite overtones of religion, reinforced by the use of church organ sounds in Paddy Kingsland's music for scenes set in the Great Book Room. The Great Book Room itself, mundanely, turns out to be the ship's bridge, but with a fanciful name and a bit of pomp the Deciders have transformed it into a ceremonial hall. Alzarian society itself is run along quasi-religious lines, with knowledge reserved for the Deciders, a mystery for the elders to be inducted into, and the ultimate knowledge of the Alzarians' origins withheld for the First Decider only. We know that Alzarius has at least one practising scientist and at least one teenage maths prodigy, which implies a larger base of scientific education, but on the whole the Alzarians that we see appear to lead a pastoral life of harvesting riverfruit, larking about in the river and submitting to the patrician authority of the Deciders. The scene in episode 1 of the Alzarians, draped in plain tunics and headscarves and carrying sacks and rough woven baskets, trudging towards the Starliner to sit out Mistfall looks like something out of a Biblical epic.

The Alzarians don't revere the Starliner in the religious sense, but they no more understand its operation than the Time Lords understand the purpose of the President's symbols of office. Unlike the Time Lords, they do at least realise that they're dealing with technology and know broadly what it's for – although how they worked that out from first principles without also working out how

---

[65] Smith, interview with author.

to use it remains a mystery – but with their limited understanding of it, it might as well be magic. Once the Doctor has helped them to master it, it becomes simply a sufficiently advanced form of technology.

Symbolic Logic

Janet Budden's set design contributes greatly to the mystical undertones of *Full Circle*. Every surface seems to have been stamped with some form of geometric shape drawn in one continuous loop. Fan publication *In-Vision* #48, the issue dealing with *Full Circle*, claims that 'Budden settled on a triangular motif for everything from doors to corridor shapes, wall monitors to bas-reliefs, tools to inspection panels'[66], but it's really only in the designs on the doors and oxygen cylinders in Dexeter's lab that this comes across; in fact the set ornamentation is dominated by complex and irregular polygrams, many of them star-shaped[67]. The most prominent shape, displayed on walls and access hatches throughout the ship, is an irregular enneagram – a nine-sided figure drawn in one loop crossing over itself – with a hexagon around it and a small equilateral triangle in the middle. Other doors and walls are adorned with large and complex patterns with seven or nine sides resembling stars with large triangular tails. Most intriguing of all is the design seen surrounding the viewscreens in the Great Book Room and the lab, an enneagram drawn in such a way that it encloses the screen in a pentagon and appears to perch a pentagram on top of it. These shapes could be taken simply as signs of continuous cyclical motion – of full circles, albeit extremely

---

[66] *In-Vision* #48, p8.
[67] Appropriately, perhaps, for a Starliner.

pointy ones – but they're also commonly seen as mystical symbols and, in the Western tradition, as symbols of magic, particularly the pentagram.

Adric's badge for mathematical excellence is a detail taken directly from the scripts, yet it strangely ties in with this aspect of Budden's set design. Functionally it was simply 'meant to mirror the marsh-reed belts that were worn by the Outlers', and in appearance it was intended as an academic 'gold star' writ large ('he's good at sums, he was top of the class for maths')[68]. As a five-pointed star, however, it also echoes these recurring stellate shapes with their magical connotations. It only needs the interior connecting lines to turn it into an overt pentagram.

The pentagram or pentangle commonly has Satanic overtones today, thanks in no small part to its appropriation by heavy metal bands everywhere and their juxtaposition of it with all manner of infernal imagery, but it was originally considered a divine symbol. Its roots can be traced back to pre-Christian times in a story recorded in the apocryphal Testament of Solomon[69]; its use as a Christian symbol is most clearly demonstrated in the Mediaeval tale of *Sir Gawain and the Green Knight*.

In this 14th-century poem, Sir Gawain's bravery and chivalry are tested as he answers the challenge laid down by the Green Knight

---

[68] Smith, interview with author.
[69] In this story, the archangel Michael gives King Solomon a ring with a five-pointed star on it – see Whittaker, M, 'The Testament of Solomon', in Sparks, HFD, ed, *The Apocryphal Old Testament*, p733. British folklorist John Aubrey described its continued use as a holy sign in the 17th century in his *Remains of Gentilism and Judaism*.

at Camelot on New Year's Day. At the start of the second canto, Gawain prepares to ride out to find the Green Knight, and his shield is brought to him. It's decorated with a gold pentangle on a red background, and the sixth and seventh verses of the canto – the 27th and 28th of the poem overall – are devoted entirely to describing the ways in which the pentangle, 'a sign that Solomon once established / As a symbol of truth', reflects Gawain's virtue. Among other sets of fivefold symbolism, particular reference is made to Gawain's faith in the five wounds of Christ on the cross and the courage he takes in battle from the five Joys of Mary[70].

By contrast, the pentagram's association with Satanism originated with the 19th century French writer Éliphas Lévi, who specified that when inverted, the pentagram represented spiritual inversion and illustrated the shape of a goat's head[71]. But the upright pentagram is still used as a sign of positive spirituality in some parts of the world today, for example on certain Mormon temples in America. Adric, the poster boy for Bidmead's scientific vision of **Doctor Who**, will walk through his 38 episodes as a companion with a magical symbol pinned to his chest, but it's a symbol that denotes his essentially good nature.

---

[70] Anon, *Sir Gawain and the Green Knight*, p45-47. The details and even the number of Mary's Joys, significant positive events in her life as Jesus' mother, vary in Catholic tradition. Online sources variously suggest any five or more from a list of as many as 15, of which only the Annunciation (the appearance of the Angel Gabriel to Mary before Jesus' birth) and the Nativity are consistently chosen.
[71] Lévi, Eliphas, *The Key of the Mysteries*, p69.

Bad Science

We might imagine that these mystical elements in *Full Circle* have been set up intentionally to be bested by the heroic force of science as championed by Bidmead. And certainly, the Doctor uncovers the truth about the Alzarians by scientific means, and at the end of the story he saves the Alzarians by gifting them technological control of the Starliner. But it's only in these moments that science is seen to triumph over mysticism, or is even presented in any kind of good light. In fact, science and technology are presented as unreliable or untrustworthy to a surprising extent in *Full Circle*.

In direct opposition to the Doctor as heroic scientist, we have Dexeter, the only visible member of Alzarius' scientific community. It's possible that Dexeter has personally evolved to mimic the original occupant of the Starliner's laboratory rather than having studied under older Alzarian scientists, but there's no clear evidence either way on this point. (It also isn't clear whether the study 'by Corellis and Dell' that he cites in episode 1 is a Terradonian one or an Alzarian one; if it was recorded in the Starliner's computer, it's quite possible it could have been written by two of the original crash survivors.) In any case, he alone represents the Scientist among the residents of the Starliner, and he's a rather unscrupulous one. He's willing not only to take tissue samples from the Marshchild but to vivisect its brain while it's awake, an operation that the Deciders have apparently endorsed and supervise from the Great Book Room. Neither Dexeter nor the Deciders are presented here as malevolent or as having any kind of sinister agenda — they're simply pursuing a line of scientific research in a completely amoral way. The Doctor raises a forceful moral objection to all of this, but is able neither to stop Dexeter nor to persuade the Deciders to accept any responsibility in the matter. An unrepentant Dexeter is killed when the Marshchild breaks free and trashes his laboratory – in a sense, it's Dexeter's own spirit of scientific inquiry that leads to his death.

Video technology in *Full Circle* is shown to be not merely unreliable, but downright deceptive. Even the TARDIS isn't exempt from this – fooled by the negative co-ordinates of E-Space, the TARDIS scanner stubbornly shows an image of Gallifrey after landing on Alzarius. Unless the TARDIS is somehow able to relay real-time visual footage from its equivalent N-Space location, it's fair to assume that the image of Gallifrey is a complete fabrication. The image translator that fixes the scanner is taken from Dexeter's microscope – a complete inversion of its function, from inspecting the interior of small things to showing the universe outside the TARDIS[72]. And the Marshchild, not understanding the technology of the Starliner's viewscreens, mistakes the image of the Doctor for the Doctor himself and is electrocuted when it tries to break through the glass to reach him.

The ill treatment of K-9 during Season 18 – blown up, kicked and generally undermined – is a comment on the behind-the-scenes feelings towards the character itself rather than a show of scepticism towards science, but his fate in *Full Circle* could be interpreted as either. Decapitated by the Marshmen in episode 2, his head is carried around as a trophy before the Doctor reclaims it and uses it as a kind of totem in episode 4. This scene is particularly striking: K-9 has habitually got the Doctor out of trouble in the past

---

[72] Or should we read something into this regarding the relative dimensions of the universe and the TARDIS?

by 'using his head', either as a repository of scientific knowledge or as a weapon, but here the Doctor uses K-9's head like a mask and invokes the character in order to play on the Marshmen's fear of the machine. The scene has the air of others in **Doctor Who** of an alien con artist playing on local superstitions by dressing up as a religious figure – K-9 the vengeful god instead of K-9 the mobile computer. It also carries a strong suggestion of shamanism, of mystics dressing in animal skins in order to invoke their spirits or to adopt their characteristics. If Tom Baker had been allowed to make barking noises in this scene as he reportedly did in rehearsals[73], the shamanic undertones of this scene would have been even stronger.

We see K-9's technological prowess fail him in his pursuit of the Marshmen in episode 2 – unable first to follow them across water[74] and then to hold them off in the cave – and now we see him transformed from a scientific object into a magical one. This looks distinctly like an expression of Bidmead's and John Nathan-Turner's recorded opinions about K-9, that by the time they took charge of the show he was being used by writers as a magical get-out for any problem the Doctor might run into.

Weird Science

Even what scientific content there is in *Full Circle* tends towards the pseudoscientific, as suggested in Chapter 2 – or even towards the parascientific. It's enough of a stretch that an earlier line of Marshmen has somehow evolved into the exact likeness of the

---

[73] DVD commentary for episode 4.
[74] Arguably the most scientifically rigorous moment in *Full Circle*, as K-9's aversion to water has a solid empirical basis in episode 1 of *The Leisure Hive*.

Terradonians[75] – one currently popular fan theory suggests that they did so simply in order to fit into the ecological niche of the Starliner[76], but this is utterly baseless. They're under no environmental pressure to do so – the Marshmen we see are already of a size and shape to live comfortably in the Starliner, and as we see, they're quite capable of learning how to open doors and operate the oxygen cylinders in the laboratory without changing physically.

But how did the Alzarians figure out the maintenance procedures for the Starliner, even with the assistance of the manual? Who taught them the language of the Terradonians that would have allowed them to read that manual in the first place? Where did they get the idea that the Starliner could and should be made to leave the surface of Alzarius? The Marshmen's continued survival doesn't depend on possessing this knowledge or these skills at all, unless they've somehow anticipated the need to fend off their successors when the next Mistfall comes round, and even then they'd be better off arming themselves with clubs and forming barricades or just staying away from the Marshman-attracting Starliner altogether. That they should undergo such unnecessary changes to their appearance and end up looking like British character actors is miraculous enough; that they should spontaneously develop the same language and the same social

---

[75] For all we know – admittedly we never see what the original Terradonians looked like. But still, let's run with that assumption for now.

[76] '...as I recently realised, the Alzarians are only humanoid because they evolved to fit inside the Starliner.' Graham, Jack, 'Things Fall Apart'.

goals as the Terradonians beggars belief. It looks for all the world as if they've simply absorbed the essence of the Terradonians from the fabric of the Starliner itself.

We're veering out of the realms of science here and into the frontiers of the paranormal – and much the same has been said about the writings of Rupert Sheldrake. It's a bit of a cheat to draw parallels between the evolutionary history of the Alzarians and Sheldrake's concept of causative formation through morphic fields – his book *A New Science of Life: The Hypothesis of Morphic Resonance* (1981) wasn't published and reviewed until after *Full Circle* had aired. Moreover, Sheldrake's website includes an exhaustive catalogue of published research papers which lists nothing on the subject prior to the publication of *A New Science of Life*[77]. It's therefore unlikely that Bidmead had read about Sheldrake's hypothesis in his *New Scientist* before *Full Circle* was transmitted, although *New Scientist* did show great interest in the subject in the years that followed[78]. Still, there are elements of *Full Circle* that seem to anticipate Sheldrake.

In *A New Science of Life*, Sheldrake proposed that experience learned by one member of a community – a flock of birds, say, or a herd of cattle – could be transferred directly to other members, notably to offspring, through something he termed 'morphic resonance' or through a 'morphic field' created by this resonance.

---

[77] Sheldrake, Rupert, 'All Scientific Research'.
[78] Notably offering a cash prize to anyone who could come up with a way of testing Sheldrake's hypothesis experimentally in volume 96 issue 1329, dated 28 October 1982, p249 ('The New Scientist – Rupert Sheldrake Prize').

He suggested that this might also extend to the transmission of physical traits, and he termed his overall hypothesis 'causative formation'. Sheldrake suggested that this might even explain such paranormal phenomena in humans as telepathy and precognition, and his later publications pursued that line of enquiry, which did nothing to ease the suspicious reception of his work by the scientific community. The hypothesis of causative formation has a superficial similarity to Lamarck's ideas about the inheritance of non-genetic characteristics, but – considered less as a scientific idea and more as a mystical one – it has far more in common with Madame Blavatsky's concept of the Akashic records[79]. These, according to Blavatsky, were a metaphysical repository of knowledge, a sort of spiritual Internet – **Doctor Who** fans might even like to think of them as a supernatural version of the Matrix[80] – that could be accessed by those with the requisite knowhow or natural ability. Blavatsky's writings were extremely popular with spiritualists around the turn of the 19th century, more or less concurrently with the heyday of Lamarckism in Anglo-American and European society.

What we see in *Full Circle* is evidence of a kind of cross-species morphic field (or Akashic record) that allowed the Alzarians to acquire the social identity and knowledge of their Terradonian victims. Perhaps they took on the appearance of the Terradonians in the same way, or perhaps it was by imitating their physical form

---

[79] Yelena Petrovna Blavatskaya (1831-91), founder of the Theosophical Society and a popular figure with spiritualists and esotericists.
[80] *The Deadly Assassin*, not William Gibson's novel *Neuromancer* (1984) or the Keanu Reeves film (1999).

that the Alzarians were able to tap into the Terradonians' morphic field in the first place.

An earlier instance in fiction of human experience being transmitted by resonance, and therefore one that Smith and/or Bidmead might actually have been aware of in 1980, is Nigel Kneale's BBC drama *The Stone Tape* (1972). In this programme – marketed as a seasonal horror story but, like *Full Circle*, with a pseudoscientific gloss – a team of scientists working for an electronics company discover that the ghostly phenomena in their isolated country retreat are really recordings of past events held in the fabric of the house, which they try to exploit in the hope of developing a new kind of recording technology. Like the Alzarians, Kneale's researchers are horrified to find themselves being pressed into repeating history by forces beyond their control.

This parascientific concept of information being recorded in the environment – built or natural – was inspired by Thomas Charles Lethbridge's paranormal non-fiction book *Ghost and Ghoul*, which was itself anticipated by Kneale's own **Quatermass and the Pit** (1958-59), in which poltergeist activity is caused by the resonance of an unearthed alien spacecraft. It may be significant that Season 18 of **Doctor Who** was overseen by Barry Letts, in the advisory capacity of executive producer, who had produced and co-authored a number of stories visibly influenced by Kneale's work during the 1970s. The idea has its roots in older paranormal concepts such as psychometry – the belief that physical objects retain an impression of people they've come into contact with – and genius loci – the belief that built or natural environments can be sentient in their own right. In the absence of any other explanation, we might look to these irrational ideas to try to rationalise the Marshmen's miraculous psychic mutation into Alzarians.

CHAPTER 5: CIRCULAR HISTORY

Decider Draith's message to Dexeter in episode 1 – 'We've come full circle' – is clearly meant to hint at the privileged knowledge of the Alzarians' origins as Marshmen that Draith possesses as First Decider, and that he hopes Dexeter as a scientist will be able to work out[81]. He presumably isn't suggesting a complete physiological 'full circle' – Alzarians mutating into Marshmen, then becoming Alzarians again – but only that the Alzarians, having once as Marshmen driven out the inhabitants of the Starliner and taken their place, now face the same fate themselves.

Despite this story's dabblings with evolutionary theory, the circle it describes is not really a biological one but a social one, albeit described through a sort of biological allegory, a strange blend of evolution and revolution. The literal rising of the Marshmen from the marsh is the uprising of a class of have-nots, disturbed by the colonisation of their world (intended or otherwise within the context of this story) by the Terradonians. Like the pigs in George Orwell's *Animal Farm* (1945), once they've seized the trappings of power from the intruders, they begin to lose their own identity and take on that of their opponents, becoming a new overclass in the image of the old. They forget their own history – in fact they suppress it, keeping it as a secret for the First Decider's eyes only – and treat the Marshmen that they themselves used to be as at best monsters, at worst subjects for experimentation. They in their turn

---

[81] He could be referring to the seasonal cycle of Mistfall, but Dexeter already knows plenty about that.

face a new uprising of Marshmen, with every prospect of history repeating itself in the new generation of Alzarians.

But this is an understanding we can only arrive at after our first viewing of *Full Circle*, when we too know the secret of the System Files. What we're initially presented with looks very much like another case of the anxiety over 'reverse colonialism' that Kate Orman identifies in **Doctor Who** and its British post-Imperial literary ancestors[82], with the invasive population of the Starliner threatened by the prospect of the Marshmen invading them right back. To recap Orman's summary, 'reverse colonialism' narratives in this line typically show 'civilisation' being threatened by an aggrieved foreign power that has been outnumbered or outgunned by the 'civilised' power but that is able to retaliate by infiltrating and corrupting its opponent, sometimes by force and sometimes by supernatural means. **Doctor Who**, with its love of body horror and of tales of possession, has occasionally made use of the latter variety of narrative to show human colonists or explorers being mentally infiltrated[83] and/or biologically corrupted[84] by alien life forms whose worlds they have encroached upon. Perversely, *Full Circle* depicts the inhabitants of the Starliner not as colonists but as crash victims, which makes it look as though all the blame for this situation rests with the aggressive natives.

At least, we're led by Nefred's pep talk in episode 2 to believe that the Starliner crashed – but who really knows? Given that the

---

[82] Orman, Kate, *The Black Archive #12: Pyramids of Mars*.
[83] As, for example, in *The Macra Terror* (1967) and *42*.
[84] Examples here include *The Ark in Space* (1975), *Planet of Evil* (1975) and *Planet of the Ood* (2008).

Starliner has been ready to take off for centuries and the only maintenance work we see being carried out is pointless make-work, perhaps the only damage to the ship was caused by the first round of Marshmen breaking in. And it is, after all, a colony ship, as Decider Garif confirms in episode 4. Perhaps the original Terradonians did come to Alzarius with the specific intention of colonising it, and the later generations of Alzarians have invented this new history for themselves.

As it turns out, the Marshmen have themselves been reverse-colonised by the environment of the Starliner, the 'primitive' weirdly corrupted by 'civilisation' in a reversal of the standard pattern for this kind of narrative.

The political system of the Alzarians as shown on screen appears to be a kind of meritocracy, with a triumvirate of Deciders apparently selected from among the populace according to the preference of their predecessors. It looks like quite an arbitrary arrangement, though. When Nefred and Garif shoulder-tap Login in episode 1 to fill the vacancy left by Decider Draith's death, their decision appears quite spontaneous; it could even be a manipulative effort to distract Login from his concern over the fact that his daughter has been shut out of the Starliner during Mistfall.

Andrew Smith's novelisation, however, offers a scenario more in line with that of Aldous Huxley's *Brave New World* (1932): Alzarians are screened at birth to decide whether they should be categorised as barely educable 'Norms' or as 'Elites' earmarked for a full scientific education, and the Deciders are chosen from among the

Elites[85]. Login is presumably therefore an Elite himself, groomed from birth for the position of authority that Nefred and Garif confer on him in such an apparently casual way. The novelisation suggests that he's 'destined perhaps one day to be a Decider'[86], although Smith doesn't specify whether that destiny was chosen for him by the incumbent Deciders or by whoever presided over his screening. We might equally well presume that Adric, as an Elite with a particular talent for mathematics, is destined to become a Decider himself.

(This detail is lost in the final version of the story as televised, in which the mention of 'Elites' is limited to the scene in episode 1 that introduces Adric. Tylos briefly reminds Varsh that they'd agreed not to allow Elites to join the Outlers; fail to hear that, and you're left only with Adric's assertion, 'Of course I'm better than you – I'm an Elite!', which sounds more like a bit of adolescent bluster than a reference to his designated social rank.)

Taken together with the teleological predicament of the Marshmen and their apparently cyclical replacement of the inhabitants of the Starliner, this all looks like a very fatalistic statement on politics: the ascension of the ruling class is a foregone conclusion, and the system is rigged to ensure their continued hold on power. Even their eventual overthrow, which is itself predetermined, is doomed only to end in more of the same.

---

[85] Smith, *Full Circle*, p7.
[86] Smith, *Full Circle*, p14.

Granted, there's no reason to suppose that *Full Circle* was ever intended to be read in this socio-political way – in fact, Smith insists that he 'just wanted to tell an adventure story':

> 'I don't try to be political [...] If people want to take that out of it, great, but it certainly wasn't a deliberate thing.'[87]

Still, it's striking that similar subject matter is openly dealt with elsewhere in Season 18, in *Warriors' Gate*, with humans and Tharils locked in a cycle of slavery and brutality. In fact, there's an interesting point of contrast between the two stories: the Alzarians have failed to learn anything from their own repeating history and seem doomed never to progress at all, whereas the Tharils have acknowledged their past as slavers and appear committed to rejecting slavery and working against it even before the Doctor intervenes. The wheel turns and brings themes of colonialism and circular history round again in the following year's *Kinda*, another script commissioned and partly shaped by Bidmead[88].

Culture and Civilisation

The teleological nature of the development of the Alzarians – socially as well as physically predetermined by the nature of the original Terradonians – and their strange shift from the hyperadaptive potential of the Marshmen to the rigid, stagnant society within the Starliner calls to mind the philosophy of human history put forward by Oswald Spengler in his two-volume work *The*

---

[87] Smith, interview with author.
[88] *In-Vision* #57, p4.

Decline of the West[89]. Rejecting the notion that students of history and the social sciences should use the same clinical methods as those working in the natural sciences, Spengler defined 'Nature' and 'History' as opposites, with Nature – spatial, causal, mathematical – being the framework within which we interpret the physical world and History – chronological, comparative rather than derived from absolute laws – being a framework within which to examine both ourselves and the world along more metaphysical lines:

> 'Nature is the shape in which the man of higher Cultures synthesizes and interprets the immediate impressions of his senses. History is that from which his imagination seeks comprehension of the living existence of the world in relation to his own life, which he thereby invests with a deeper reality.'[90]

A conventional view of history might describe an event in terms of its proximate causes and effects and the interactions between its participants – a rational, even mathematical approach that, said Spengler, 'would be nothing but a piece of "natural science" in disguise'[91]. By contrast, he advised extending the study of historical events along temporal rather than spatial lines and attempting by analogy with other events to glimpse the overall shape of human history. Spengler's view of history was:

---

[89] Spengler, Oswald, *The Decline of the West, Volume One: Form and Actuality* (1922) and *The Decline of the West, Volume Two: Perspectives of World-History* (1926).
[90] Spengler, *Form and Actuality*, p8.
[91] Spengler, *Form and Actuality*, p6.

'...not as a mere sum of past things without intrinsic order or inner necessity, but as an organism of rigorous structure and significant articulation, an organism that does not suddenly dissolve into a formless and ambiguous future when it reaches the accidental present of the observer'[92].

Indeed, his aim as stated in the opening sentence of *The Decline of the West* was, by describing the shape of this history-organism, to attempt 'the venture of predetermining history'[93].

Developing his metaphor, Spengler broke down the life cycle of his history-organism into the following stages, based on his consideration of a number of ancient and modern societies. First is the stage from which Culture[94] coalesces, a loosely connected pre-urban society concerned only with its immediate existence. Then comes Culture itself, a more urbanised society in which science, art and other lines of inquiry and self-exploration flourish, and the defining character of the society — which Spengler calls its 'world-feeling'[95] — begins to emerge. The next stage is Civilisation, more centralised and more analytical than Culture, the stage at which the society becomes more fixed and inward-looking and focuses on its 'world-feeling' to the exclusion of all other possible worldviews:

---

[92] Spengler, *Form and Actuality*, p104.
[93] Spengler, *Form and Actuality*, p3. The umbrella title of his duology gives a pretty broad hint as to his conclusions.
[94] All nouns are capitalised in German, but Spengler's translator Charles F Atkinson opted to keep the initial capitals for 'Culture' and 'Civilisation' in this particular context because Spengler defined the two concepts in a very specific way, and so I've capitalised them too.
[95] Spengler, *Form and Actuality*, p14 and passim.

'Every Culture stands in a deeply symbolical, almost in a mystical, relation to the Extended, the space, in which and through which it strives to actualize itself. The aim once attained – the idea, the entire content of inner possibilities, fulfilled and made externally actual – the Culture suddenly hardens, it mortifies, its blood congeals, its force breaks down, and it becomes Civilisation...'[96]

Finally the Civilisation reaches for the ultimate expression of its 'world-feeling', either to impose it on everyone else or simply to pass it down to posterity, expends itself and falls into decline. Spengler saw this progression as linear and unavoidable, the decline of any society and the path it must take through Culture and Civilisation to get there being predetermined. He elaborated on this in terms of 'destiny' rather than the more scientific 'teleology', describing teleology as 'a caricature of the Destiny-idea'[97], but in any case there's a clear parallel between this view of cultural development as following a predetermined course and the way that Alzarian culture has developed along a course entirely predetermined by that of the Terradonians.

The concepts of Culture and Civilisation, which are central to Spengler's philosophy of history, are strongly if unintentionally reflected in *Full Circle*. The Marshmen certainly fit the description of Culture quoted above: they stand in an almost mystical relation to the world in which they exist, and we can see in their determined march to the Starliner and their assault on it that they don't adapt passively but are actively striving to actualise

---

[96] Spengler, *Form and Actuality*, p106.
[97] Spengler, *Form and Actuality*, p120.

themselves. If the Marshmen represent Culture, then the Alzarians are Civilisation, static and stagnant, ossifying out of the mutable and inquisitive Culture, defining themselves and their purpose but in the process losing the wealth of possibilities they previously had.

CHAPTER 6: TEENAGE KICKS

It is a truth universally acknowledged that Christopher H Bidmead came up with the name 'Adric' as an anagram of the surname of mathematician Paul Dirac[98]. Dirac is sometimes credited as having predicted the existence of antimatter, which isn't strictly true – rather, his mathematical work raised questions that were later resolved when physicists were able to demonstrate the existence of antimatter. In looking for a name for the character of a maths prodigy from another universe, it's natural that Bidmead should have thought of Dirac.

Dirac formulated the equation that bears his name in 1928 as a sort of bridge between quantum mechanics and special relativity[99]. Schrödinger's quantum theory predicted the behaviour of electrons in relation to atomic nuclei in a way that worked on paper but didn't match what particle physicists were seeing in the lab. The Dirac equation resolved the discrepancies but created new problems of its own, the chief one being that it opened up the

---

[98] For the sake of argument, let's cite Pixley, 'DWM Archive: Full Circle'.
[99] Dirac, PAM, 'The Quantum Theory of the Electron'. *Proceedings of the Royal Society A* volume 117 issue 778, 1 February 1928. Interested readers can find this paper online (see Bibliography for details) – I don't want to give away the twist ending, but let's just say it involves eigenstates.

possibility of particles with the same mass as an electron but with a balancing positive charge. Four years later Carl David Anderson observed such a particle, which he named the positron[100]. All of a sudden the concept of antimatter, previously the subject of fanciful speculation among physicists, had become mainstream science. In the meantime, Dirac had suggested that the problem might be solved if the role of these anti-electrons were taken on by 'holes' in the quantum vacuum behaving as if they had a positive charge[101].

E-Space isn't presented as a universe of antimatter[102], but it is presented as an inverse of the regular universe, with negative spatial co-ordinates. Mathematics – Dirac's equation – predicts the existence of an E-Space to balance the Doctor's N-Space and, as we find out at the end of Season 18, it's the mathematical wizards of Logopolis who've opened the way to E-Space by creating a pocket of charged vacuum, something not far removed from Dirac's idea of a quantum 'hole' which here becomes a literal hole in the universe that the TARDIS falls through.

The Microchip (R)evolution

Adric's name may be inspired by Dirac, but the inspiration for his character lies elsewhere. The outline drafted by Bidmead and John

---

[100] Anderson, Carl David, 'The Positive Electron'.
[101] Dirac, PAM, 'A Theory of Electrons and Protons'. *Proceedings of the Royal Society A* volume 126 issue 801, 1 January 1930.
[102] **Doctor Who** already had ideas of its own about what an antimatter universe should look like – see *The Three Doctors* (1972-73).

Nathan-Turner in early 1980 compares him to the Artful Dodger[103] but apart from his youth and his occasional moments of thievery, the two characters aren't very similar. Adric has more in common with the teenage mathematical geniuses of Silicon Valley who had created a mass market for affordable home computers just a few years earlier. Bidmead, an early adopter and enthusiast of home computers, would surely have read about and admired the entrepreneurial hackers who'd created his own beloved Vector Graphic MZ System B.

The hacker ethos, as expressed by the pioneers of home computing[104] and their predecessors, is that people should be permitted every access to the hardware and software that make computing possible, so that they can find their own uses for it. In its earliest days in the 1960s, hacker culture was focused around the Massachusetts Institute of Technology (MIT) and was decidedly elitist – the early hackers, with their devotion to the exploration of computing for its own sake, considered themselves better than

---

[103] The pseudonym of Jack Dawkins, leader of a juvenile criminal gang in Charles Dickens' *Oliver Twist* (1839, originally serialised 1837-39). Dawkins' age is never given in the book, although he's presumed to be around Oliver's age, which would put him in his pre-teens; his unchildlike behaviour could reflect the rough circumstances of his childhood, or could suggest he's actually older than he seems. On screen, he's typically been played by actors between the ages of 16 and 18, a closer match for Matthew Waterhouse's age in 1980.

[104] Notwithstanding Bill Gates' contention that programmers should be able to make a living by exercising copyright over their code, which served him well financially but put him at odds with many of his hacker peers.

their non-mathematical peers or the cadre of trained but unadventurous operators who'd been given exclusive use of the IBM computers at MIT, which the hackers described as a 'priesthood'[105].

Adric, let's not forget, is 'an Elite' – he doesn't question whether or not he's better than his peers, he simply asserts it[106], and his rejection of the authority of the priest-like Deciders suggests he feels the same way about those who claim guardianship of the Starliner and its secrets. He readily aligns himself with the anarchic, hackerish Doctor, who breaks the Deciders' exclusive hold over the records of Alzarian history – tellingly referred to as the System Files, a computing term that describes files containing information necessary to the proper working of a computer system – and shows them how to make full use of the machinery at their disposal.

The TARDIS might be thought of as a kind of computer – it's presented increasingly in those terms during the 1980s, with pop-up keyboards and BBC Micro graphic displays suddenly appearing on the control console[107] – and as such it's a natural target for Adric's attention. As a hyperadaptive 'hopeful monster' with an affinity for numbers, he might even see an ideal habitat in an environment that, as it turns out in *Logopolis*, has been constructed entirely through mathematics. It isn't until *Earthshock* that we see Adric using the TARDIS console to calculate a return trajectory into

---

[105] Levy, Steven, *Hackers: Heroes of the Computer Revolution*, p24 and passim.
[106] *Full Circle*, episode 1.
[107] Note also sundry recent references in scripts written by Steven Moffat to the decor of the TARDIS console room as its 'desktop theme'.

E-Space – actually hacking out a program on a computer – but the Doctor is willing to explain the workings of the ship to him in *Logopolis*, and it's clear in his debut story that he feels entitled to explore it and meddle with it, managing (accidentally) to launch it in episode 2 and (as we later discover) stowing away in it at the end of the story.

Having adapted to his new habitat, we might imagine Adric in true Alzarian fashion changing to mimic the dominant life form: the Doctor himself. It wouldn't be the first time the companion character had turned apprentice Doctor – this was practically the starting point for Romana, who ends up defying the order to return to Gallifrey and acting as E-Space's very own heroic rogue Time Lord at the end of *Warriors' Gate*. Nor would it be the last – Clara exits the series in *Hell Bent* (2015) having stolen a TARDIS from Gallifrey; and had **Doctor Who** not been taken off the air in 1989, it had been mooted that Ace would have been written out in a story in the 1990 season that would see the Doctor enrolling her in the Time Lord Academy[108].

We noted in Chapter 4 that Adric was not originally intended to mirror the Doctor in any way, but that hasn't stopped Matthew Waterhouse from suggesting that some of the scriptwriters, and more recently the writers of the Big Finish audio dramas, depicted Adric as a sort of imitation Doctor by giving the two characters similar speech patterns:

---

[108] Owen, Dave, '27 Up', DWM issue 255, p10. This story idea was later adapted as the Big Finish audio drama *Thin Ice* (2011), not to be confused with the **Doctor Who** TV story *Thin Ice* (2017).

'[I]t's a conscious choice by the writers because of course he hero-worships the Doctor and in some ways is a younger version of the Doctor, and so he actually speaks like the Doctor rhythmically.'[109]

Any potential pay-off to this line of character development, if it ever existed, was lost at the end of Season 18 when Bidmead left **Doctor Who**. Subsequent writers and script editors increasingly wrote Adric as a generic companion, albeit with an unwarranted fixation on his interest in mathematics, until his sudden exit from the series in *Earthshock*.

Adric – The Undertones

Readers might be startled by the suggestion that there was ever anything fashionable about Adric, but whether by accident or design, something of British pop culture at the end of the 1970s does seem to have influenced his appearance. A comment – or a criticism – that's often made about **Doctor Who** in the early 1980s is that the lead characters' costumes started to look more like uniforms, artificial and unchanging. This may have been related in some way to John Nathan-Turner's various efforts to position the show as a marketable commodity domestically and overseas, but it also seems to echo what was happening in the popular music scene around the end of the 1970s. Punk rock had presented a front of open rebellion against the mainstream musical establishment during its popular peak in the mid-70s, but that peak was followed by a wave of artists looking to challenge the establishment in more experimental ways. One strain of these post-punk bands chose to

---

[109] *Myth Makers* #129.

mock the music industry by visually emphasising the manufactured nature of their music, often wearing identical business suits in concert but sometimes wearing more unusual uniforms.

Among what would become the 1981 TARDIS crew, Adric most clearly resembles this variety of post-punk musician, his yellow tunic and trousers particularly calling to mind the yellow radiation suits worn by American band Devo. His hairdo, however – and given that this was a wig when Waterhouse started working on **Doctor Who** in *State of Decay*, we should view it as a deliberate choice[110] – is reminiscent of an altogether different style of musician: it's an uncanny match for the untidy mop of Paul Weller, who was enjoying chart success with his band The Jam around that time and who became a figurehead for the British mod revival of the late 70s and early 80s.

By comparing **Doctor Who** visually with the BBC's now defunct pop chart show **Top of the Pops** (1964-2006), we can chart a relationship between **Doctor Who** and the contemporary music scene. It's at its most obvious during the period from the mid-60s – when psychedelic imagery became a significant element in British pop – to the early 80s, when professionally produced pop videos were becoming commonplace. The directors of **Top of the Pops** would typically liven up a programme full of studio performances with the same experimental video effects then in use on **Doctor**

---

[110] The DVD production subtitles for *Full Circle* state that Matthew Waterhouse had grown out his own hair during his month off after filming *State of Decay* and was then sporting his own hair, but in his memoir *Blue Box Boy* Waterhouse mentions wearing a wig during location filming for *Full Circle* at Black Park (Waterhouse, Matthew, *Blue Box Boy* pp136, 145).

Who: the assorted camera distortion effects of the 70s, Quantel in the early 80s. But beyond this, the costumes and set design of **Doctor Who** would routinely reflect the musical 'look' of the day as explored on **Top of the Pops**, the behind-the-scenes personnel striving to make both programmes appear as futuristic as possible: the Op Art and monochrome psychedelia of the 60s, the lurid glam rock stylings of the early 70s. **Doctor Who** during the early 80s was visually more in line with the New Romantic movement that was burgeoning at the start of the decade[111]; but at the time *Full Circle* was made the field of pop culture in punk rock's wake was still broad, diverse and undecided, and Adric's melange of cultural influences reflects that.

Teenage Takeover

But Adric was intended more generally to behave like a teenager and to provide a viewpoint character for the teenage members of the audience. He's almost a caricature – surly, self-opinionated, rebellious, always hungry – and it's not clear how much of this came from the story's own teenage scriptwriter, how much from the production team via Adric's character outline, how much from the actor's interpretation of the character, and how much these aspects of the character were embellished by the writers of

---

[111] Adric dresses up in a very New Romantic buccaneer costume in *Black Orchid* (1982); see also the buccaneer costumes of Lon in *Snakedance* (1983) and Wrack's crew in *Enlightenment*, the somewhat whimsical historical costumes on display in *The Visitation* (1982) and *The King's Demons* (1983), and of course Traken, the Planet of the New Romantics.

subsequent stories. Andrew Smith doesn't deny that he drew on his own experiences at that time in shaping the character:

> 'I always hesitate to say this, but I was kind of top of the class and good at maths and English and things, and I think there was quite a lot of me certainly in the Adric in *Full Circle*.'[112]

Much was made at the time of the fact that both the scriptwriter and the new companion actor were teenagers, with *Radio Times* leading press interest on the subject[113]. Matthew Waterhouse came to **Doctor Who** directly from recording **To Serve Them All My Days** (1980-81), in which he played the minor part of bereaved schoolboy Briarley in the first two episodes, but that programme didn't debut until the week before episode 1 of *Full Circle* was transmitted, so at that time Waterhouse was still an unknown quantity as an actor. He'd auditioned for and won the role of Adric before filming on **To Serve Them All My Days** had even started. He was 18 years old when he made his screen debut, celebrating his 19th birthday between the transmission of *State of Decay* and *Warriors' Gate*. Andrew Smith, who turned 18 during the location filming for *Full Circle*, had enjoyed some prior success contributing material to radio and TV comedy sketch shows and had sent a number of script proposals to the **Doctor Who** production office before being commissioned for *Full Circle*. He still holds the unique distinction of being the only teenage writer to have been formally commissioned by the **Doctor Who** production office[114]. *Radio Times* described the

---

[112] Smith, interview with author.
[113] 'Teenage takeover in 'Doctor Who'?', *Radio Times* issue 2972.
[114] He's also unusual in having been a self-described **Doctor Who**

story as the teenagers' 'big break', and this flurry of interest in their employment on the show must have made it seem as though the production team were not just trying to appeal to viewers in that age group but trying moreover to present **Doctor Who** as the kind of vibrant, up-to-the-minute programme that encouraged new talent.

This was far from the first time a teenage actor had been cast in a principal role on the show. Jackie Lane was 18 and Deborah Watling 19 when they debuted on screen as Dodo Chaplet and Victoria Waterfield[115], and it was commonplace during the 1960s for the show to include at least one regular character of presumably adolescent age, even though such characters were more often played by actors in their 20s. However, during the 1970s the show had adopted a more 'grown-up' tone. Jon Pertwee's run showed the influence of such whimsical action series as ABC's **The Avengers** (1961-69) and often trod similar ground to the BBC's own contemporary **Doomwatch** (1970-72), both of which played later in the evening to an older audience than **Doctor Who**. The early years of Tom Baker's run, which included several horror movie parodies, would also seem to be part of this overt attempt to appeal to older viewers. Accordingly, the Doctor's companions had become more grown-up too. Since 1970, it had been the norm for the Doctor to be accompanied by one companion – apart from the brief inclusion

---

fan at the time of his commissioning – one of the first, but far from the last fan to have realised his dream of working on the show. The history of fannish involvement in the making of **Doctor Who** is briefly considered in the Appendix.

[115] In *The Massacre* (1966) and *The Evil of the Daleks* (1967) respectively.

in Tom Baker's first year of Harry Sullivan, whose chief purpose was to handle the rough-and-tumble action scenes if the new lead actor should prove unable to do so – and that one companion was usually female and in her 20s, or apparently so[116]. Waterhouse's casting was thus of interest in that he was playing the first overtly adolescent companion in a decade, and the first male companion since Harry more than five years earlier.

Following Adric's introduction, teenage companions became a common sight in **Doctor Who** once more. Waterhouse was followed onto the show almost immediately by 19-year-old Sarah Sutton playing Nyssa[117], and subsequent companions included Turlough, masquerading as a schoolboy[118] even though the actor playing him was clearly in his 20s; Peri, a university student, which most fan writers and commentators have taken to mean that she was 18 or 19 when she met the Doctor[119]; the extremely teenage Ace[120]; Rose Tyler[121]; and – in their late teens during most of *The Eleventh Hour* (2010) – Amy Pond and Rory Williams.

Teenage characters beyond the TARDIS crew aren't so easy to find, however, and *Full Circle* is notable for its large and prominent

---

[116] Admittedly there's no clear evidence either way as to how old Leela was supposed to be, beyond Louise Jameson being in her mid-20s at the time.
[117] *The Keeper of Traken*.
[118] *Mawdryn Undead*.
[119] *Planet of Fire* (1984). And you won't find any helpful clues from looking at her passport, according to which she's 43 years old and answers to the name of Sydney.
[120] *Dragonfire* (1987).
[121] *Rose* (2005).

contingent of teenagers in the form of the Outlers, Alzarius' own disaffected youth counterculture. It's no coincidence that this age group should be so well-represented and play such a key role in Andrew Smith's debut TV script. (Their role was even greater in the first draft of episode 4, which would have ended with the Outlers at the helm of the Starliner as it took off; this was changed in Bidmead's second draft rewrite[122].) Also notable is the fact that the Outlers include Keara, the only female speaking part other than series regular Romana in an otherwise male-dominated story. Adric and his peers are presented as being more perceptive and more daring than their elders, but caught in the same cycle of events and no less subject to the same threats. Significantly, among the Marshmen the lone juvenile character of the Marshchild serves much the same function. In early drafts of the story, the Marshchild had a larger role which extended as far as playing the part of a temporary assistant to the Doctor[123]; once Smith was commissioned and the character of Adric was introduced into his story, the Marshchild's role diminished accordingly.

The only significant teen character to appear after this in Season 18 is Nyssa; Season 19 includes such lone examples as the unnamed child in *Castrovalva* and Panna's apprentice Karuna in *Kinda*, but we don't see another instance of multiple secondary adolescent characters on screen until Season 20's *Mawdryn Undead* (1983).

Even today, while adult and pre-teen characters are well represented in **Doctor Who**, it's relatively unusual to see a teenager in a major primary or secondary role; spin-off series **The Sarah Jane**

---

[122] Smith, interview with author.
[123] Pixley, 'DWM Archive: Full Circle'.

Adventures (2007-11) and the more 'young adult' **Class** (2016) both revolve around a core cast of teenagers[124], but the parent show seems less inclined to appeal to this section of the audience through on-screen representation.

---

[124] Perhaps surprisingly in the case of **The Sarah Jane Adventures**, since that programme was produced for the children's channel CBBC and was thus ostensibly targeted at pre-teens and their parents rather than at adolescents.

CHAPTER 7: THE CREATURE FROM THE BLACK PARK LAGOON

By their nature as fantasy melodrama, **Doctor Who** stories tend to revolve around the interaction between 'monsters' and 'victims', the latter usually human and the former more often than not inhuman. *Full Circle* treats its Alzarian and Marshman characters with a certain degree of equitability, showing particularly in the case of the Marshchild how human (or apparently human) characters can behave like monsters towards their inhuman victims. But the other purpose of 'monsters' in **Doctor Who** is to provide a bit of visual spectacle, and on that score fandom seems comfortably settled in its opinion that the Marshmen are this story's monsters[125].

The Marshmen are unusual as monsters in **Doctor Who**, and in science fiction more generally, even apart from the sympathetic way in which they're portrayed by comparison with the Alzarians. It's common enough for monsters to turn their human victims into copies of themselves, and there are plenty of examples of monsters disguising themselves as humans in order to get closer to their victims, but it's rarely heard of for the victims to turn out, to their own surprise, to have formerly been monsters.

The idea of intelligent, non-human beings posing as humans for their own benefit has its roots in folkloric stories of changelings, supernatural creatures – sometimes infants themselves, but more usually older beings capable of speech and reasoned thought – left

---

[125] See, for example, Miles and Wood's assessment that 'the good monsters are back!' (*About Time 5*, p36).

in the cradles of newborns to be cared for at the expense of unsuspecting human parents. Internet sources suggest that there are instances of tales in which the changeling forgets its origin and believes itself to be human, but provide no verifiable citations. However, changeling stories describe an exchange rather than a straightforward infiltration, with a corresponding human child being abducted by the supernatural community; they are also concerned with individuals rather than with the replacement of an entire populace.

The myth of the changeling was given an overhaul in the mid-20th century in science fiction stories about alien shapeshifters, the flagship examples being John W Campbell's novella *Who Goes There?* (1938), first (loosely) adapted for film as *The Thing from Another World* (1951), and Jack Finney's *The Body Snatchers* (1955), first filmed as *Invasion of the Body Snatchers* (1956). In these stories, the replacement of humans with impostors is destructive rather than an exchange, the aliens consuming their victims in order to take on their form and persona. Their ultimate goal is similarly destructive: their own reproduction and continuation depends on them taking over the world at the cost of humanity's extinction, starting with the isolated community of an Antarctic research station in *Who Goes There?* and through an all-out global assault in *The Body Snatchers*. This is closer to, if still not a good match for, the behaviour of the Marshmen in *Full Circle*; although the Marshmen take on the appearance of the Terradonians after killing them, they do so apparently in reaction to their surroundings rather than as part of a deliberate scheme to conquer Terradon.

It's easy to spot the difference in ideologies behind these stories. The 'body snatcher' stories are part of the first flush of Cold War paranoia in American culture, *Who Goes There?* being published three months after the establishment of the House Committee on Un-American Activities to investigate suspected domestic political subversion, and *The Body Snatchers* being originally serialised in *Colliers Magazine* in its 26 November, 10 December and 24 December editions, debuting after Senator Joseph McCarthy's fall from grace in popular opinion but a week before his censure by the Senate on 2 December. Scenes of human characters revealing their alien identities or being murderously replaced reflect the contemporary fears of political undesirables, usually Communists, infiltrating American society or of citizens being seduced and subverted by America's own Communist Party or similar organisations. *Full Circle* is concerned not with the horror of society being politically undermined by foreign powers, but rather with the horror of learning that there's no material difference between the society being defended and the threat it's being defended against.

A related fear among Americans during the Cold War was that of 'sleeper agents': outsiders posing as conventional Americans in order to assume strategically useful positions in society, or Americans brainwashed by enemy agents, conditioned to respond to a predetermined trigger and act on given orders without their own knowledge or consent. There are numerous real-world examples – proven or suspected – of the first kind of sleeper agent, but the second kind is more popular in fiction, the touchstone example being Richard Condon's political thriller *The Manchurian Candidate* (1959). Science-fiction stories followed of alien infiltrators conditioned to believe themselves to be human, a notable recent example in the **Doctor Who** universe being the **Torchwood** (2006-11) episode *Sleeper* (2008). But again, in these examples it's an individual who's been compromised rather than the whole community.

A more benign variation can be seen in **Doctor Who**'s *The Zygon Invasion / The Zygon Inversion* (2015), which features alien impostors who've assumed the form and personalities of human originals simply in order to live peacefully among humans. The character of Osgood in particular expresses her desire for peaceful integration by refusing to disclose whether she's human or Zygon. This story differs from *Full Circle* in that the impostors know that they're not really human, and drama is created from the human characters addressing the fact that they're living alongside Zygons rather than from fear that they themselves might be Zygons.

The closest match for *Full Circle* in terms of how its monsters relate to their victims is Gene Wolfe's book *The Fifth Head of Cerberus* (1972). This collection of three novellas is set on the twin colony worlds of Sainte Anne and Sainte Croix, the former of which was once inhabited by a species of shape-changing hominids. In the first of the three novellas, the majority of the human settlers believe that the native shape-changers have died out, but in the third novella a human anthropologist – the suggestively-named Marsch – encounters an apparent survivor and is seemingly replaced by him. The second novella, an account of the life of the native species, is presented as a story written by Marsch, ostensibly a piece of academic whimsy that in hindsight starts to look more like his replacement's memoir; one of the tribes encountered by the protagonist of Marsch's story is referred to as 'the marshmen'.

Wolfe doesn't offer much in the way of definite answers – in this or his other books – but he does offer a strong hint as to the fate of the shape-changers of Sainte Anne in the first novella. Here we're told about 'Veil's Hypothesis', a piece of wild speculation presented in a scientific format, which suggests that the shape-changers not only survived among the human settlers but learned to imitate them so perfectly that they took on the physiology and personalities of the colonists, to the extent of losing their own personalities and their ability to change shape in the process. The author of Veil's Hypothesis goes so far as to suggest that the inhabitants of Sainte Anne and Sainte Croix are actually all natives who've killed and replaced the human colonists.

Swamp Thing

In appearance, the Marshmen have often been compared to the Creature from the Black Lagoon, the star of three Universal Pictures films and the last of the iconic Universal monsters. Gary Hopkins made this comparison shortly after the programme's transmission in *The Doctor Who Review* issue 8 (1980)[126], and similar comments have been made about the Marshmen and about the scene of their emergence from the marsh in reviews, interviews and critical analyses ever since. Andrew Smith recalls making a similar connection when he attended the location filming in Black Park in Buckinghamshire; after first being surprised that the costumes didn't match his own conception of the Marshmen, '[m]y second thought was, it's the Creature from the Black Lagoon'[127].

---

[126] Quoted in Howe, David J, and Stephen James Walker, *Doctor Who: The Television Companion* (1998) (pp388-89), which is in its turn quoted on the BBC's webpage '**Doctor Who**: The Classic Series – *Full Circle*'. It's recursion all over again!
[127] Smith, Andrew, DVD commentary, episode 2.

The Creature – more properly referred to as the Gill-man – debuted in *Creature from the Black Lagoon* (1954), coming several years after the heyday of Universal's monster movies but proving popular enough to justify the sequels *Revenge of the Creature* (1955) and *The Creature Walks Among Us* (1956).

The physical similarity between the Gill-man and the Marshmen isn't particularly strong, beyond their scaly, amphibious skin. Facially they're very different, the Marshmen having rounded faces with narrow eyes and no lips while the Gill-man's head is domed and sports prominent, piscine lips and eyes. Even the scene of the Marshmen emerging from the water at the end of episode 1 has no obvious parallel in any of the *Creature* films[128]. All three films fully reveal the Gill-man in underwater shots and feature numerous scenes of him fighting his human opponents while still in the water before showing him on land; none of them features a dramatic scene of him striding out of the water. The nearest equivalent is a shot just two minutes from the end of the original *Creature*, in which the Gill-man erupts from a misty pool to attack the film's male human lead, and this is played for a quick shock rather than for any visual spectacle.

Smith has consistently stated in interviews that he envisaged the Marshmen as being more like cave-men[129], and the rehearsal scripts for the story describe them as 'horrible half-men half-

---

[128] It does, however, have an obvious parallel in episodes 3 and 4 of The Sea Devils (1972).
[129] See, for example, *Myth Makers* #122 and the DVD commentary for episode 2.

beasts'[130]. They were, however, always referred to as 'Marshmen', a name more suggestive of the final costume design than of hominids. Matthew Waterhouse recalls that *Creature from the Black Lagoon* was a fixture at a 3-D cinema in Soho at that time, easily within reach of anyone working at the BBC[131]. It could thus have been an influence on costume designer Amy Roberts, who should be credited with the creation of the Marshmen's physical appearance. But equally, given that the figure of the Gill-man has passed into popular culture far beyond the limits of his own films, Roberts could have been influenced by him unconsciously rather than directly. Smith suggests that a certain similarity between the Gill-man and Roberts' final design was inevitable:

> 'I don't think it's lifted from that, maybe subliminally, but if you're looking at designing a creature that lives underwater [...] you're maybe automatically going to finish up with something that looks like the Creature [from the Black Lagoon].'[132]

It's interesting to chart the deeper connections between the two creatures. In *Creature*, the Gill-man is discovered in South America by a team of geologists and biologists looking for fossil evidence of an amphibious 'missing link'. An unexpected and apparently lone survivor of a prehistoric age, the Gill-man reacts badly to the intrusion of the human scientists into his territory but is clearly

---

[130] Pixley, 'DWM Archive: Full Circle'.
[131] Waterhouse, *Blue Box Boy*, p165. Although he may have meant the second film, *Revenge of the Creature*, which was filmed in 3-D and exploits the device in a number of gimmicky shots.
[132] Smith, interview with author.

attracted to the one female member of the expedition, stalking her when she goes swimming and eventually abducting her. He's shot several times at the end of the film and sinks back into the lagoon, but as he recovered spectacularly from injuries sustained earlier in the film, it's not too surprising that he should survive to reappear in the sequels.

The Gill-man's remarkable healing faculties are an obvious point of comparison with life on Alzarius, and although there's no suggestion in the first film that he can 'evolve' as fast (or at all) as a relic of the mid-Paleozoic Era, he's practically the polar opposite of the mutable Marshmen – the third film in the series offers some surprising revelations on the subject. He certainly doesn't seem to want to join or supplant the team of human scientists that's entered his domain, but his infatuation with human women – a running feature of his films – suggests some desire on his part to integrate into human society. Like the Marshmen, he's seen as a threat by the other characters but presented as essentially sympathetic, only acting violently because his territory has been invaded[133]. Unlike the Marshmen, the Gill-man only seems to attack humans if they attack him first, but as the Marshmen are shown to learn by observing and copying the actions of others, it's unclear to what extent their aggression is innate or was caused by interaction with the original Terradonians. Crucially, like the Marshmen, the character of the Gill-man stands for the existential, even Gothic horror of evolutionary theory as applied to humans – a 'missing

---

[133] In the Marshmen's case, the invasion happened generations earlier when the Terradonians first arrived on Alzarius, and the generation of Marshmen we see are reacting rather to the continued presence of the Starliner.

link' come back to terrorise us. He's the only Universal monster to be inspired by contemporary science rather than by folklore or classic literature[134].

Revenge is little more than a retread of the first film with a change of scenery. The Gill-man is captured and brought to an aquarium in mainland America where he predictably falls for a female scientist, breaks free and causes chaos; he finally disappears underwater after being repeatedly shot. *The Creature Walks Among Us* starts off on familiar territory, but after a leisurely first half hour it heads off in a startling new direction. During an attempted recapture the Gill-man is badly burned and the human scientists take him on board their boat where they have the medical facilities needed to treat him. The injuries to his gills and scales are severe, but his captors are astonished to discover that he has rudimentary lungs and a layer of smooth, human-like skin underneath his scorched epidermis. They perform a tracheotomy to help him breathe, give him clothes to wear and intend to help him adapt to a new life on land while keeping him under house arrest in California. Things go wrong when the Gill-man is framed for a murder among the scientists, and after taking his revenge on the murderer he escapes

---

[134] Despite its scientific trappings, for Universal Pictures *Frankenstein* (1931) was simply another adaptation of a classic horror novel to follow their smash hit *Dracula* (1931). Victor Frankenstein's experiments, the nature of which is left vague in Mary Shelley's novel, were inspired by the practice of galvanism – stimulating the muscles of dead animals with electricity – which was contemporary to Shelley and based on scientific principles, but generally used for the purpose of sensationalist public entertainment.

to the coast where he presumably commits suicide by drowning in the water he can no longer breathe in.

In this third film, the Gill-man is presented as far more of a sympathetic character than before, even a tragic one, and although he shows no enthusiasm for his new life among the humans, it's remarkable that he's able to adapt to it physiologically so quickly and so radically. More superficially this new, air-breathing Gill-man bears more of a physical resemblance to the Marshmen, the head of his new costume being more rounded and the eyes hooded. Of the three *Creature* films, it's the third one that offers the strongest echoes of *Full Circle*'s Marshmen.

Despite his apparent death at the end of each film, the Gill-man still lived on in one sense or another. When his own film sequels dried up, he found a new career as a bit-part comedy character; his first major role after *The Creature Walks Among Us* was as Uncle Gilbert in an episode of **The Munsters** (1964-66), *Love Comes to Mockingbird Heights* (1965), and his IMDb page lists a variety of other appearances since then.

We don't see what happens to the Marshmen after they leave the Starliner in episode 4. Perhaps they're left milling about where it used to be, looking for a new habitat to move into. Perhaps, unlike the unfortunate Gill-man, they're able to re-adapt to life underwater. Perhaps, with the Starliner gone, they're reabsorbed into the body of the planet – a fate that would fit with Smith's original concept of life on Alzarius. Smith's novelisation seems to chart an ambiguous course between these latter two possibilities:

'As one, the creatures entered the marshlands, sinking beneath its surface, disappearing under the murky slime – until it was as if no one had ever been there[135].'

---

[135] Smith, *Full Circle*, p62.

APPENDIX: POACHERS TURNED GAMEKEEPERS

Doctor Who has a long and noble history of reaching out to its fans, encouraging them to think about how the show is made and to engage actively with it. At the simplest level of engagement, numerous books, magazine articles and behind-the-scenes programmes have offered an insight into the process of making **Doctor Who**, providing an informative resource for inquisitive fans[136]. More directly, the Doctor Who Fan Club, precursor to the present-day Doctor Who Appreciation Society, enjoyed the patronage and active support of the Pertwee-era production office under Barry Letts between 1971 and 1976[137]. The fans returned this support during the 70s and 80s by offering reference material and advice to subsequent producers, mostly with regard to maintaining the show's longer-term continuity.

The impact of this fan outreach on the writing of **Doctor Who** in the 20th century was fairly minimal. The only scriptwriters who were avid fans of the show at the time of their commissioning, as we would understand the word 'fan', were Andrew Smith and some of the writers commissioned by Andrew Cartmel in the late 80s, such as Ben Aaronovitch[138] and Marc Platt[139]. These writers notably brought an awareness of the show's history and of science fiction

---

[136] As noted in Chapter 1, one of the books Andrew Smith referred to when teaching himself the rudiments of writing for television was Dicks and Hulke's *The Making of Doctor Who*.
[137] Hearn, Marcus, *Doctor Who: The Vault*, p124.
[138] *Remembrance of the Daleks* (1988) and *Battlefield*.
[139] *Ghost Light*.

and fantasy tropes in general to their **Doctor Who** scripts. Beyond these few instances, there are only the continuity references scattered across the scripts of 80s **Who**, any of which might have been prompted by a suggestion from unofficial fan consultant Ian Levine or other fans. We might not wonder that it took 17 years for the first generation of **Doctor Who** fans to be represented among the show's scriptwriters, or indeed among its leading cast[140]. It is perhaps more surprising that it should have taken a further eight years for another overtly fannish writer to be commissioned.

The turning point in putting **Doctor Who**'s reins in the hands of its fans came during the lengthy 'Wilderness Years' period encompassing the years between *Survival* (1989) and *Rose* (2005). In the television series' absence between these stories (*Doctor Who* (1996) excepted), fans took it upon themselves to continue the **Doctor Who** franchise in a variety of media including comic strips, audio dramas and, perhaps most pertinently, the spin-off novel series published by Virgin Books (1991-97) and BBC Books (1997-2005), as well as embellishing the extended universe of the show through an assortment of unlicensed video and audio dramas. Since **Doctor Who**'s relaunch in 2005, the majority of episodes have been scripted by writers who had previously contributed to the tie-in books, including showrunners Russell T Davies and Steven

---

[140] Although time probably isn't the only consideration there; as Bernard Padden recalls in 'All Aboard the Starliner', at that time 'it wasn't done to [work] on **Doctor Who** and say you were a fan'.

Moffat[141]. The show has even featured the celebrity **Doctor Who** fans David Tennant and Peter Capaldi in the title role.

And these 'poachers turned gamekeepers' have used their position to enthuse the next generation of **Doctor Who** fans. The 21st century has seen a very high degree of engagement between fans and programme makers, most notably through a variety of **Blue Peter** (1958-present) competitions that have allowed fans direct access to the production process. In 2005, **Blue Peter** ran a competition to design a monster for **Doctor Who**, similar to one they'd run in 1967 but with the difference that this time the winning entry would actually be featured in an episode of the show[142]; similar competitions in 2006 and 2010 provided opportunities for an aspiring child actor to appear in an episode[143], and for an artistic fan to design a new TARDIS console to be featured briefly on-screen[144]. All three competition winners were given an on-screen credit for their contribution to the relevant episodes and at least one of them, actor John Bell, has since turned professional in the same field.

---

[141] Admittedly, half of the episodes have been written or co-written by the incumbent showrunner, which skews the figures somewhat. For footnote completists: Davies wrote the novel *Damaged Goods* (1996) and Moffat wrote a short story for *Decalog 3: Consequences* (1996).

[142] *Love & Monsters* (2006), whose villain, the Abzorbaloff, had been designed by nine-year-old William Grantham.

[143] John Bell, who was cast in the role of Creet in *Utopia* (2007) at the age of nine.

[144] The junkyard TARDIS console seen in *The Doctor's Wife*, as designed by 12-year-old Susannah Leah.

More recently, the 'Script to Screen' competition overseen by BBC Learning and **Doctor Who Confidential** (2005-11) in parallel with Series 6 in 2011 gave young fans the chance to write a four-minute story to be broadcast nationwide. The winners were regularly featured on **Confidential** during the second half of Series 6, following their script through the production process, and the finished minisode was broadcast as part of the final episode of **Confidential**[145]. The competition was run again the following year, with **Blue Peter** transmitting the winning story[146]. Although neither instance constitutes the formal commissioning of a **Doctor Who** story, both of the 'Script to Screen' stories were filmed using the resources of the **Doctor Who** production office and televised by the BBC, and both arguably have as much claim to legitimacy as part of the paratext of **Doctor Who** as any of the many other minisodes created in connection with the show in recent years[147].

Of course, the passage of time is a factor in this increase in fannish engagement in recent decades. With more than 50 years of history behind it, **Doctor Who** will naturally have been more widely seen and have gathered more fans than it could have at the time Andrew Smith was commissioned to write *Full Circle*. De facto, the proportion of people working on **Doctor Who** who are likely to describe themselves as fans, or to remember having watched the

---

[145] 'Death is the Only Answer' (2011), written by pupils of Oakley Junior School.
[146] 'Good as Gold' (2012), by pupils of Ashdene School.
[147] 'Good as Gold' was included as an extra on the UK release of the Series 7 DVD box set alongside eight minisodes by professional writers. 'Death is the Only Answer' remains unreleased at time of writing.

show during their formative years, is higher today than it was in 1980. Viewed in this light, Smith's commissioning back then might appear all the more extraordinary; but taken in the broader historical context of the willingness of producers and script editors to interact with aspiring fannish creators – witness the encouragement Smith recalls receiving from Robert Holmes, Anthony Read and Douglas Adams as well as Christopher Bidmead during his early forays into scriptwriting[148] – it looks more like the first step in an inevitable fan inrush.

---

[148] *Myth Makers* #122 and 'All Aboard the Starliner'.

BIBLIOGRAPHY

Books

Anon, *Sir Gawain and the Green Knight* (*Sir Gawayn and þe Grene Knyȝt*). 14th century. WS Merwyn, trans, Hexham, Bloodaxe Books Ltd, 2003. ISBN 9781852246341.

Aristotle, *A History of Animals* (*Tōn Peri ta Zōa Historiōn*). Fourth century BCE. D'Arcy Wentworth Thompson, trans, Oxford, Clarendon Press, 1910.

Asimov, Isaac, *Foundation's Edge*. New York, Doubleday, 1982. ISBN 9780385177252.

Aubrey, John, *Remains of Gentilism and Judaism, 1686-87*. 1881. Montana, Kessinger Publishing, 2010. ISBN 9781167214547.

Bonnet, Charles, *Considerations sur les corps organisés*. Amsterdam, Marc-Michel Rey, 1762.

Bucher-Jones, Simon, *Image of the Fendahl*. **The Black Archive** #5. Edinburgh, Obverse Books, 2016. ISBN 9781909031418.

Campbell, John W, *Who Goes There?* 1938. USA, Rocket Ride Books, 2009. ISBN 9780982332207.

Campbell, Mark, *Doctor Who: The Episode Guide*. **The Pocket Essential**. 2000. Harpenden, Pocket Essentials, 2011. ISBN 9781842436608.

Clarke, Arthur C, *Profiles of the Future*. 1962. London, Pan Books Ltd, 1973. ISBN 9780330236195.

Condon, Richard, *The Manchurian Candidate*. 1959. London, Orion Books, 2013. ISBN 9781409147800.

Darwin, Charles, *On the Origin of Species by Means of Natural Selection, or the Preservation of Favoured Races in the Struggle for Life*. 1859. London, Penguin Books, 2009. ISBN 9780140439120.

Darwin, Charles, *The Descent of Man, and Selection in Relation to Sex*. 1871. London, Penguin Books, 2004. ISBN 9780140436310.

Darwin, Erasmus, *Zoonomia: Or, the Laws of Organic Life*. 1796. London, J Johnson, 1801.

Dawkins, Richard, *Climbing Mount Improbable*. London, WW Norton & Co, 1996. ISBN 9780393039306.

Dickens, Charles, *Oliver Twist, or, The Parish Boy's Progress*. 1838. London, Penguin Books, 2003. ISBN 9780141439747.

Eimer, Theodor, *On Orthogenesis and the Impotence of Natural Selection in Species-Formation*. 1897. Montana, Kessinger Publishing, 2008. ISBN 9781437029666.

Finney, Jack, *The Body Snatchers*. 1955. London, Gollancz, 2010. ISBN 9780575085312.

Goldschmidt, Richard, *The Material Basis of Evolution*. Connecticut, Yale University Press, 1940.

Gould, Stephen Jay, *Ontogeny and Phylogeny*. Cambridge, Harvard University Press, 1977. ISBN 9780674639416.

Haacke, Wilhelm, *Gestaltung und Verebung: Eine Entwickelungsmechanik der Organismen* (‚Formation and Heredity: an Evolutionary Mechanism of Organisms'). 1893. London, Forgotten Books, 2016. ISBN 9781332367962.

Haeckel, Ernst, *Generelle Morphologie der Organismen* ('General Morphology of Organisms'). Berlin, G Reimer, 1866.

Hearn, Marcus, *Doctor Who: The Vault*. London, BBC Books, 2013. ISBN 9781849905817.

Howe, David J, and Mark Stammers, *Doctor Who: Companions*. London, Virgin Publishing, 1995. ISBN 9781852275822.

Howe, David J, and Stephen James Walker, *Doctor Who: The Television Companion*. London, BBC Books, 1998. ISBN 9780563405887.

Hulke, Malcom, *Writing for Television in the 70's*. London, A & C Black, 1974. ISBN 0713614692.

Hulke, Malcolm and Terrance Dicks, *The Making of Doctor Who*. London, Pan Books, 1972. ISBN 0330232037

Huxley, Aldous, *Brave New World*. 1932. London, Flamingo, 1994. ISBN 0586044345.

Lamarck, Jean-Baptiste, *Zoological Philosophy: An Exposition with Regard to the Natural History Of Animals* (*Philosophie Zoologique: Ou Exposition des Considérations Relatives à l'Histoire Naturelle des Animaux*). 1809. Hugh Samuel Roger Elliot, trans, London, Macmillan & Co, 1914.

Lem, Stanisław, *Solaris*. 1961. Joanna Kilmartin and Steve Cox, trans, New York, Walker, 1970. ISBN 9780156027601.

Lethbridge, TC, *Ghost and Ghoul*. London, Routledge 1961. ISBN 9780710061911.

Lévi, Éliphas, *The Key of the Mysteries* (*La Clef des grands mystères suivant Hénoch, Abraham, Hermès Trismégiste et Salomon*). 1861. Aleister Crowley, trans, London, Rider & Company, 1959.

Levy, Steven, *Hackers: Heroes of the Computer Revolution*. 1984. California, O'Reilly Media Inc, 2010. ISBN 9781449388393.

Lovelock, James, *Gaia: A New Look at Life on Earth*. 1979. Oxford, Oxford University Press, 2000. ISBN 9780192862181.

Magner, Lois N, *A History of the Life Sciences*. Third ed. New York, Marcel Dekker Inc, 2002. ISBN 9780824708245.

Miles, Lawrence, and Tat Wood, *1980-1984: Seasons 18 to 21*. **About Time: The Unauthorized Guide to Doctor Who** #5. Illinois, Mad Norwegian Press, 2005. ISBN 0975944649.

Oparin, AI, *The Origin of Life* (*Vozniknovenie Zhizni na Zemle*). 1924. Sergius Morgulis, trans, New York, Dover Publications, Inc, 1953. ISBN 9780486495224.

Orman, Kate, *Pyramids of Mars*. **The Black Archive** #12. Edinburgh, Obverse Books, 2017. ISBN 9781909031579.

Orwell, George, *Animal Farm*. 1945. London, Penguin Books, 1951. ISBN 0140008381.

Osborn, Henry Fairfield, *From the Greeks to Darwin: An Outline of the Development of the Evolution Idea*. New York, Macmillan & Co, 1905.

Reynolds, Simon, *Rip It Up and Start Again: Post-punk 1978-84*. London, Faber and Faber, 2005. ISBN 9780571252275.

Sheldrake, Rupert, *A New Science of Life: The Hypothesis of Morphic Resonance*. 1981. Vermont, Park Street Press, 1995. ISBN 9780892815357.

Shelley, Mary, *Frankenstein; or, The Modern Prometheus*. 1818. London, Penguin Books, 1995. ISBN 9780140433623.

Smith, Andrew, *Doctor Who: Full Circle*. **The Target Doctor Who Library** #26. London, W H Allen, 1982. ISBN 9780426201502.

Sparks, HFD, ed, *The Apocryphal Old Testament*. Oxford, Clarendon Press, 1984. ISBN 9780198261773.

> Whittaker, M, 'The Testament of Solomon'.

Spengler, Oswald, *The Decline of the West, Volume One: Form and Actuality* (*Der Untergang des Abendlandes, Erster Band: Gestalt und Wirklichkeit*). 1918, revised 1922. Charles F Atkinson, trans, New York, Alfred A Knopf, Inc, 1926.

Spengler, Oswald, *The Decline of the West, Volume Two: Perspectives of World-History* (*Der Untergang des Abendlandes, Zweiter Band: Welthistorische Perspektiven*). 1922. Charles F Atkinson, trans, New York, Alfred A Knopf, Inc, 1928.

Waterhouse, Matthew, *Blue Box Boy*. 2010. London, What Noise Productions, 2013. ISBN 9780956853974.

White, Andrew Dickson, *A History of the Warfare of Science with Theology in Christendom*. 1896. London, D Appleton & Co, 1922.

Wolfe, Gene, *The Fifth Head of Cerberus*. 1972. London, Gollancz, 1999. ISBN 9781857988178.

Periodicals

Doctor Who Magazine (DWM). Marvel UK, Panini, BBC, 1979-.

> DWM Special Edition #16: *In Their Own Words – Volume 3 – 1977-81*, cover date July 2007.

> Owen, Dave, '27 Up'. DWM #255, cover date August 1997.

Pixley, Andrew, 'DWM Archive: Full Circle'. DWM #327, cover date March 2003.

Pixley, Andrew, 'Archive Extra'. DWM Special Edition #9: *The Complete Fourth Doctor – Volume 2*, cover date December 2004.

Spilsbury, Tom, 'Graeme Harper'. DWM #380, cover date

In-Vision. Cybermark Services, 1988-2003.

Season 16 Overview. #38, June 1992.

The Leisure Hive. #46, September 1993.

Meglos. #47, November 1993.

Full Circle. #48, January 1994.

State of Decay, #49, March 1994.

Warriors' Gate. #50, April 1994.

Kinda. #57, May 1995.

Proceedings of the Royal Society A (PRSA). Royal Society Publishing, 1905-.

Dirac, PAM, 'The Quantum Theory of the Electron'. PRSA volume 117 issue 778, 1 February 1928.

Dirac, PAM, 'A Theory of Electrons and Protons'. PRSA volume 126 issue 801, 1 January 1930.

'Teenage Takeover in **Doctor Who**?', *Radio Times* issue 2972, 23 October 1980.

'The New Scientist – Rupert Sheldrake Prize', *New Scientist* volume 96 issue 1329, 28 October 1982.

Anderson, Carl David, 'The Positive Electron'. *Physical Review* volume 43 issue 6, 15 March 1933.

Gould, SJ, 'Return of the Hopeful Monster'. *Natural History* volume 86 issue 6, June-July 1977.

Lee, Stan, Jack Kirby, Vince Colletta and Sam Rosen, 'Rigel – Where Gods May Fear to Tread!'. *Thor* volume 1 #132, September 1966.

Miller, Stanley L, 'Production of Amino Acids Under Possible Primitive Earth Conditions'. *Science*, volume 117 issue 3046, 15 May 1953.

Moore, Alan, Dave Gibbons and Anthony Tollin, 'Tales of the Green Lantern Corps: Mogo Doesn't Socialize'. *Green Lantern* volume 2 #188, May 1985.

Television

The Avengers. ABC Weekend Television, 1961-69.

Blue Peter. BBC, 1958-.

Callan. ABC Weekend Television, Thames Television, 1967-72.

Class. BBC, 2016.

Count Dracula. BBC, 1977.

Doctor Who. BBC, 1963-.

    Full Circle. DVD release, 2009.

        'All Aboard the Starliner'. DVD extra.

        'E-Space: Fact or Fiction?' DVD extra.

Doctor Who Confidential. BBC, 2005-11

Doomwatch. BBC, 1970-72.

Edge of Darkness. BBC, 1985.

    'Magnox: The Secrets of Edge of Darkness'. DVD extra, 2003.

The Munsters. CBS Television Network, Kayro-Vue Productions, 1964-66.

    Love Comes to Mockingbird Heights, 1965.

Public Eye. ABC Weekend Television, Thames Television, 1965-75.

Quatermass and the Pit. BBC, 1958-59.

The Sarah Jane Adventures. BBC, 2007-11.

Star Trek: The Next Generation. Paramount Television, 1987-94.

    Genesis, 1994.

The Stone Tape. BBC, 1972.

To Serve Them All My Days. BBC, 1980-81.

Top of the Pops. BBC, 1964-2006.

Torchwood. BBC, 2006-11.

    Sleeper, 2008.

Film

Arnold, Jack, dir, *Creature from the Black Lagoon*. Universal International Pictures, 1954.

Arnold, Jack, dir, *Revenge of the Creature*. Universal International Pictures, 1955.

Barnfather, Keith, dir, **Myth Makers**. Reeltime Pictures, 1984-.

Christopher H Bidmead. #87. Reeltime Pictures, 2006.

Andrew Smith. #122. Reeltime Pictures, 2016.

Matthew Waterhouse. #129. Reeltime Pictures, 2017.

Gunn, James, dir, *Guardians of the Galaxy Vol. 2*. Marvel Studios, 2017.

Nyby, Christian, dir, *The Thing from Another World*. RKO Radio Pictures, Winchester Pictures Corporation, 1951.

Sherwood, John, dir, *The Creature Walks Among Us*. Universal International Pictures, 1956.

Siegel, Don, dir, *Invasion of the Body Snatchers*. Walter Wanger Productions, 1956.

Tarkovsky, Andrei, dir, *Solaris*. Mosfilm, 1972.

Whale, James, dir, *Frankenstein*. Universal Pictures, 1931.

Web

'The Creature from the Black Lagoon (Character)'. IMDb. http://www.imdb.com/character/ch0021218/. Accessed 15 August 2017.

'**Doctor Who**: The Classic Series – *Full Circle*'. BBC One: **Doctor Who**, 24 September 2014. http://www.bbc.co.uk/doctorwho/classic/episodeguide/fullcircle/. Accessed 15 August 2017.

Clarke, Paul, '*Full Circle*'. *Doctor Who Reviews*, 31 December 2003. http://reviews.doctorwhonews.net/2003/12/full_circle1314.html Accessed 12 September 2017.

Dirac, PAM, 'The Quantum Theory of the Electron'. Royal Society Publishing. http://rspa.royalsocietypublishing.org/content/117/778/610. Accessed 15 August 2017.

Graham, Jack, 'Things Fall Apart'. *Shabogan Graffiti*, 9 November 2011. http://shabogangraffiti.blogspot.co.nz/2011/11/things-fall-apart.html. Accessed 14 December 2017.

Sheldrake, Rupert, 'All Scientific Research'. http://www.sheldrake.org/research. Accessed 15 August 2017.

BIOGRAPHY

In 1980, John Toon was a child maths prodigy with a dodgy haircut; today he is a bearded science mystic. He was one of the founding contributors to *The Professor X Programme Guide*, an online **Doctor Who** parody in the 1990s, but he's learned his lesson and he's very sorry. He celebrated **Doctor Who**'s 50th anniversary by blogging about the electronic soundtracks of the 50 stories broadcast during the 1980s (http://doctorwhoelectronica.blogspot.co.nz/). He and his partner emigrated from the UK eight years ago to New Zealand, where he has become a prominent participant in the science fiction fan community. He likes comics, Godzilla and expressing himself through the medium of cosmetics. This is his first book.